The George Foreman®

Next Grilleration™ *G5 Cookbook*

**Inviting & Delicious Recipes
for Grilling, Baking, Waffles,
Sandwiches & More!**

Deb Roussou

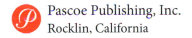 Pascoe Publishing, Inc.
Rocklin, California

Published in the United States of America by

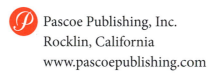 Pascoe Publishing, Inc.
Rocklin, California
www.pascoepublishing.com

ISBN: 1-929862-51-2

06   07   08   10   9   8   7
Printed in China

Table of Contents

Introduction & Basic Cooking Tips  4

Chapter 1 — *Appetizers* 7

Chapter 2 — *Breakfast—Waffles, Pancakes, Eggs, Potatoes & More* 14

Chapter 3 — *Lunch—Panini, Quesadillas, Sandwiches & More* 36

Chapter 4 — *Salads & Sides* 51

Chapter 5 — *Dinner Entrées — Beef, Lamb & Pork* 68

Chapter 6 — *Dinner Entrées—Chicken, Seafood & Vegetarian Dishes* 79

Chapter 7 — *Marinades, Sauces & Rubs* 97

Chapter 8 — *Desserts* 106

Chapter 9 — *Basic Cooking Guide* 114

Index 118

Introduction

SUMPTUOUSLY FLAVORED, YET QUICKLY PREPARED, your introduction to delectable breakfast dishes, satisfying luncheon fare and exotic dinner entrées is within the pages of this exciting, new cookbook. If you enjoy flavor combinations that delight the palate—ethnic dishes with a touch of Americana, delicious seafood with fresh herb sauces, homemade waffles with fruit butters and grilled meats with tantalizing accompaniments, the recipes inside this book were created for you.

The "art" of food preparation has changed over the past years as the ever-quickening pace of our lives has changed. Savoring the taste of exquisitely prepared foods has moved from being the highest priority to often being the lowest, as we search for the most convenient and fast way to prepare our meals. But, the introduction of the George Foreman® The Next Grilleration™ G5 can change that outlook. With a patented heating system and 5 interchangeable plates, you can easily grill, bake, waffle and sauté all of your favorite recipes and more—in record time!

For breakfast, try *Breakfast Tacos*, crispy *Apple Ginger Waffles* and scrumptious *French Toast with Strawberry Butter*. Scramble a few eggs, grill some bacon and serve it with *Crispy Hash Browned Potatoes* in less than half the time it would take on the stovetop. For lunch, pop the Steak Plate into the George Foreman® The Next Grilleration™ G5 and try the *Chevre, Fig & Proscuitto Panini*, a healthy *Albacore Tuna Melt* or a *Crab & Avocado Quesadilla*. Dinner entrée choices may include *Stuffed Chile Rellenos*, *Chicken Piccata*, *Island Jerked Pork with Lime Crème Fraîche*, or *Grilled Japanese Vegetables with Wasabi Butter*. The tantalizing tastes of a new world await your knife, fork and spoon.

The George Foreman® The Next Grilleration™ G5 is designed with a lever to allow the grill to either move to the front position for lowfat grilling, or to be moved to the back position for baking or flat pan cooking. When sloped, the fat is channeled away from foods as they cook on the grill. This prevents foods from sitting in fat and absorbing unnecessary calories. When the G5 is in the back position, the flat surface enhances the quality of cooking foods such as pancakes, waffles and eggs.

The interchangeable plates of the George Foreman® The Next Grilleration™ G5 are coated with a special nonstick surface that allows you to beautifully brown and grill foods without the added calories and fat of butter or oil. When you plan to grill foods that can stick to the plates, such as food coated with a marinade that contains honey or sugar, you may want to lightly spray the grill plates with non-stick cooking spray.

The George Foreman® The Next Grilleration™ G5 is equipped with a temperature control that lets you grill foods to perfection. When preparing food, set the temperature to a Low, Medium or High setting as directed in the recipes and use the *Basic Cooking Guide* in the back of this book as a handy reference. The temperatures and times suggested are only guidelines, as food cooking times can vary due to the thickness of the food or other variables.

The heating elements in the George Foreman® The Next Grilleration™ G5 cook both sides of your food at once, cutting typical cooking times in half. Foods are grilled fast and evenly so there is no need to turn your food as it cooks.

Always close the George Foreman® The Next Grilleration™ G5 when cooking. When cooking food in batches on the High setting, open the grill and let it cool for a few minutes between every 2 or 3 batches. This will help ensure that the grill does not become too hot for the proper cooking temperature.

Follow the manufacturer's instructions carefully when using the drip trays, spatulas and other grilling accessories. Use only heat-resistant plastic spatulas on the nonstick grilling and plate surfaces.

When checking meats, fruits and vegetables for doneness, carefully insert the tip of a sharp knife into the foods. Do not cut all the way through the food or touch the grill with the knife, as it will scratch the nonstick surface.

Use caution when opening the heated grill, as the plates are hot. Children should not touch or use the grill while assisting with food preparation. They should not stand near the grill or sit on the kitchen counter when the grill is in operation.

Follow the manufacturer's instructions to safely clean your grill. Clean the grill housing properly each time you use it and do not use harsh cleansers or steel scouring pads. Remove the cooled grill plates as directed, wash in warm soapy water with a soft sponge or cloth, and rinse thoroughly. Dry the plates and place them in the grill.

Appetizers

APPETIZERS, OR "LITTLE BITS OF SAVORY GOODNESS" as they are often called, are generally the stars of the show at a cocktail party, formal dinner party, or when served together to form a casual meal. It is simple to create appealing lowfat appetizers—even a cucumber round with a slice of smoked salmon and a dollop of lowfat cream cheese can create the mood and flavor experience you crave.

The trick to appetizers is to engage your family and friends in the introduction to the meal. Serve appetizers that complement the meal, avoiding repetitive tastes or flavors that will be served in the main course. A common temptation is to serve cheeses with assorted crackers—which is not altogether a bad idea, however if your main course is laden with cheese, you will want to re-think whether or not additional cheese should be a part of the appetizer course. Choose appetizers that will enhance the flavors of the main meal rather than compete with it.

The recipes in this chapter are inventive and are offered as a way to invite your own creativity—*Grilled Bacon-Wrapped Shrimp, Keema Kebabs with Mango Chutney Dipping Sauce*, and *Grilled Polenta with Duo Olive Tapenade*. Recipes from Chapter 4 can also be served as appetizers—*Greek Chicken Orzo Salad* or *Grilled & Chilled Seafood Salad.* Enjoy a delicious and promising beginning to any meal!

Curried Corn Cakes

These tasty fritters make a great appetizer or a wonderful
accompaniment with grilled meats or fish.

1½ cups	all-purpose flour
1½ teaspoons	baking powder
2 teaspoons	curry powder
1½ teaspoons	salt
1 cup	liquid egg substitute
¼ cup	fat-free half and half
⅓ cup	lowfat margarine, melted
1¼ cups	fresh or frozen yellow corn kernels
¼ cup	nonfat sour cream
4	green onions, chopped
	nonstick cooking spray

In a medium bowl, combine the flour, baking powder, curry and salt, mixing well to blend. Add the egg substitute, half and half and melted margarine, stirring until the flour mixture is just moistened. Do not overmix. Gently stir in the corn.

Place the Steak Plate in the top of the grill and the Baking Pan in the bottom. Set the lever to the back. Set the temperature to High to allow the grill to preheat. When the green light goes off, the grill is preheated. Spray the top and bottom Plates with nonstick cooking spray. Spoon 4 to 6 spoonfuls of batter onto the grill, close the lid, and cook for 4 minutes. Check the fritters and continue cooking until the center is firm and the outside edges are browned. Repeat with any remaining batter. Serve with a dollop of sour cream and a sprinkling of green onions.

Serves 4.

Calories: 209

Total Fat: 4g

Saturated Fat: 1g

% Calories from Fat: 15

Carbohydrates: 35g

Protein: 10g

Cholesterol: 2mg

Sodium: 898mg

Grilled Bacon-Wrapped Shrimp

This is a 70's classic and a proven crowd pleaser.

4 slices	bacon
8 large	shrimp, shelled and deveined, tails on
½ cup	fresh pineapple, cut into 1-inch cubes, (substitute canned pineapple chunks)
2	8-inch wooden skewers, soaked in water and drained

Place the Steak Plate in the top of the grill and the Grilling Plate in the bottom. Set the lever to the front. Set the temperature to High to allow the grill to preheat. When the green light goes off, the grill is preheated. Place the bacon strips in the grill, close the lid, and cook for 5 minutes. Remove the partially cooked bacon to paper towels. When the bacon is cool enough to handle, cut the bacon strips in half crosswise. Wrap each shrimp in a piece of bacon and thread onto the skewer, alternating with a pineapple chunk, placing 4 shrimp on each skewer.

Set the temperature to High to allow the grill to preheat. When the green light goes off, the grill is preheated again. Place the skewers in the grill horizontally, close the lid and cook for 2 to 3 minutes. Check the shrimp with the tip of a knife and continue grilling until the shrimp is pink and no longer opaque.

Serves 2.

Calories: 169

Total Fat: 10g

Saturated Fat: 4g

% Calories from Fat: 53

Carbohydrates: 5g

Protein: 14g

Cholesterol: 73mg

Sodium: 582mg

Keema Kebabs with Mango Chutney Dipping Sauce

The cool, sweet-tart dipping sauce complements the spicy, savory flavors of the lamb kebabs. Serve as an appetizer or stuff into pita bread for a quick lunch.

1 pound	ground lamb
1	shallot, finely diced
2 cloves	garlic, finely minced
1½ teaspoons	ground cumin
1 teaspoon	ground turmeric
1 teaspoon	salt
1½ teaspoons	garam masala
¼ teaspoon	chili powder
3 tablespoons	fresh cilantro, finely minced
1	egg, lightly beaten
4 or 5	10-inch wooden skewers, soaked in water and drained

Combine the ingredients in a medium bowl, mixing well to blend. Place a sheet of plastic wrap on the counter. Working on the plastic wrap, mold the lamb mixture around the skewers to form flattened sausages, about 6 to 8 inches long and ½-inch thick. Place the Steak Plate in the top of the grill and the Grilling Plate in the bottom. Set the lever to the back. Set the temperature to Medium to allow the grill to preheat. When the green light goes off, the grill is preheated.

Carefully lift the kebabs and place in the grill horizontally. Close the lid and cook for 6 to 7 minutes. Check the lamb with the tip of a knife and continue grilling for 1 to 2 minutes, if necessary. Place the skewers on a serving platter and serve with *Mango Chutney Dipping Sauce.*

Serves 4. ❧

Mango Chutney Dipping Sauce

2 tablespoons	lowfat sour cream
2 tablespoons	lowfat plain yogurt
2 teaspoons	mango chutney

In a small bowl, make the sauce by combining the sour cream, yogurt and chutney, mixing well to blend. Cover the bowl tightly with plastic wrap and refrigerate until needed.

Serves 4. ∾

Calories: 385

Total Fat: 28g

Saturated Fat: 12g

% Calories from Fat: 66

Carbohydrates: 11g

Protein: 21g

Cholesterol: 137mg

Sodium: 681mg

Homemade Grilled Crostini

Homemade grilled crostini is a simple appetizer, but the flavors of fresh-roasted garlic and herbs are incomparable. Grill extra garlic to have on hand for soups, pasta dishes and salad dressings.

1	Italian baguette, sliced into ½-inch thick rounds
1 head	garlic
2 tablespoons	extra-virgin olive oil
1 teaspoon	dried ground basil
1 teaspoon	dried ground thyme
1 teaspoon	dried ground oregano

Place the Steak Plate in the top of the grill and the Grilling Plate in the bottom. Set the lever to the back. Set the temperature to High to allow the grill to preheat. When the green light goes off, the grill is preheated. Place the baguette slices in the grill in a single layer, close the lid, and grill for 1 minute. Check the crostini and continue grilling, for 1 to 2 minutes, if necessary, until golden brown.

Separate the garlic cloves and cut off the tough end that was connected to the head, but leave the papery skins intact. Place in a small bowl, add the oil and herbs and toss to coat.

Place the Steak Plate in the top of the grill and the Baking Pan in the bottom. Set the lever to the back. Set the temperature to Medium to allow the grill to preheat. When the green light goes off, the grill is preheated. Place the unpeeled garlic cloves in the Baking Pan, close the lid and cook for 7 minutes. Check the garlic and continue cooking until the garlic is very soft and warm. Gently squeeze the garlic from the papery skin into a small serving bowl. Smooth a very thin layer of garlic over each crostini and serve.

Serves 4. ❧

Calories: 228

Total Fat 3g

Saturated Fat: <1g

% Calories from Fat: 11

Carbohydrates: 42g

Protein: 7g

Cholesterol: 0mg

Sodium: 457mg

Grilled Polenta with Duo Olive Tapenade

Find prepared polenta in tubes in the specialty section of your grocery store. Try plain or flavored polenta and experiment with your own family favorites.

24 ounce	tube prepared sun-dried tomato-flavored polenta
2 tablespoons	extra-virgin olive oil
1 cup	Duo Olive Tapenade (see p. 39)

Slice the polenta into ½-inch thick slices. Place the Steak Plate in the top of the grill and Grilling Plate in the bottom. Set the lever to the back. Set the temperature to Medium to allow the grill to preheat. When the green light goes off, the grill is preheated. Lightly brush the polenta slices with the oil and place in the grill in a single layer. Close the lid. Cook for 2 to 3 minutes. Check the polenta and continue grilling until scored and golden brown. Place a small serving bowl of *Duo Olive Tapenade* in the center of a serving platter and surround it with grilled polenta slices.

Serves 12.

Calories: 289

Total Fat: 12g

Saturated Fat: 2g

% Calories from Fat: 37

Carbohydrates: 39g

Protein: 7g

Cholesterol: 4mg

Sodium: 591mg

Breakfast

Waffles, Pancakes, Eggs, Potatoes & More

REAKFAST IS THE START OF THE DAY—the promise of a new beginning. If you want to begin your day with a serving of hearty goodness, try *Croissant French Toast with Warm Berries, Caper-Dill Waffles with Smoked Salmon Cream Cheese* or *Red Flannel Hash*. If you prefer to begin the day with a lighter touch, look for recipes such as *Pumpkin Soufflé Pancakes* or *Breakfast Rice Cakes* and add a glass of freshly-squeezed juice.

Many of the heavily sweetened breakfast treats that are considered classics—waffles, pancakes and French toast, can take a lighter role as you prepare them with warm fruit, lowfat spreads and fruit butters. Lowfat doesn't have to mean boring and these recipes prove that point well!

Simply Scrambled Eggs

Sunny scrambled eggs are a snap in the George Foreman® The Next Grilleration™ G5.
Fifty seconds is all it takes—and that includes melting the margarine!

4	eggs
½ teaspoon	salt
½ teaspoon	black pepper
2 teaspoons	lowfat margarine

In a medium bowl, whisk the eggs with the salt and pepper. Place the Steak Plate in the top of the grill and the Baking Pan in the bottom. Set the lever to the back. Set the temperature to Medium to allow the grill to preheat. When the green light goes off, the grill is preheated. Place the margarine in the grill, close the lid and let the margarine melt for 30 seconds. Pour the eggs into the grill, close the lid and cook for 10 seconds. Open the grill and scramble well. Close the lid and cook for an additional 10 seconds or until done, according to your preference.

Serves 2. ❧

Calories: 159

Total Fat: 11g

Saturated Fat: 3g

% Calories from Fat: 64

Carbohydrates: 2g

Protein: 13g

Cholesterol: 425mg

Sodium: 744mg

Bacon & Eggs, Your Way

Imagine no more spattered mess; just crispy bacon and eggs your way!

4 pieces	smoked turkey bacon
2	eggs
½ teaspoon	black pepper

Place the Steak Plate in the top of the grill and the Baking Pan in the bottom. Set the lever to the back. Place the bacon in the grill. Set the temperature to High and close the lid. Grill the bacon for 10 to 13 minutes. Transfer the bacon, using a heat-resistant plastic spatula, to paper towels to drain. Break the eggs into the grill and dust with pepper. Close the lid and cook for 1 minute. Open the grill and flip the eggs. Close the lid and cook according to your preference: 1 minute for over-easy eggs, 1½ minutes for over-medium eggs, and 2 minutes for over-hard eggs. Transfer the eggs to individual plates and serve with crispy bacon.

Serves 2. ❧

Note: For a lower fat option, place the Grilling Plate in the bottom and set the lever to the front. Cook the bacon for 7 to 8 minutes on High, allowing the fat to drip away from the bacon into the drip pan. Transfer the bacon to paper towels to drain. Allow the grill to cool slightly and change the bottom grill to the Baking Pan. Set the temperature to High and preheat. Cook the eggs as instructed above.

Serves 2. ❧

Calories: 148

Total Fat: 10g

Saturated Fat: 3g

% Calories from Fat: 62

Carbohydrates: 3g

Protein: 11g

Cholesterol: 233mg

Sodium: 443mg

Breakfast Tacos

A southern breakfast staple, now found on breakfast tables in all parts of the country. Vary the taco fillings to suit your own preferences and enjoy!

6	eggs
1 teaspoon	salt
1 teaspoon	black pepper

Choose 2 or more of the following ingredients:

¼ cup	cooked lowfat sausage, crumbled
¼ cup	cooked turkey bacon, crumbled
2	green onions, finely chopped
¼ cup	canned green chiles, chopped
¼ cup	white potatoes, cooked
¼ cup	lowfat Monterey Jack cheese, grated
¼ cup	lowfat longhorn cheddar cheese, grated
¼ cup	prepared salsa
4 large	nonfat flour tortillas
2 tablespoons	lowfat margarine

In a medium bowl, whisk together the eggs with the salt and pepper. Add 2 or more ingredients from the above list and whisk to blend. Place the Steak Plate in the top of the grill and the Baking Pan in the bottom. Set the lever to the back. Set the temperature to Medium to allow the grill to preheat. When the green light goes off, the grill is preheated.

Place 2 tortillas in the grill at a time, close the lid, and heat for 40 seconds. Transfer to a plate and cover with foil. Repeat with the remaining tortillas. Place the margarine in the grill, close the lid and let the margarine melt for 30 seconds. Pour the eggs into the grill, close the lid and cook for 20 seconds. Open the lid and scramble well. Close the lid and cook for an additional 20 seconds, or until done according to your preference.

Place equal portions of the eggs into the 4 warm tortillas and serve with additional salsa, if desired.

Serves 4. ❧

Calories: 238

Total Fat: 13g

Saturated Fat: 3g

% Calories from Fat: 48

Carbohydrates: 15g

Protein: 16g

Cholesterol: 332mg

Sodium: 1081mg

Omelet Lorraine

Because the new George Foreman® The Next Grilleration™ G5 cooks both sides at once,
it is easy to cook this fluffy, cheesy omelet without flipping!

4	eggs
¼ teaspoon	baking powder
2 tablespoons	fresh thyme, chopped (substitute 2 teaspoons dried thyme)
1 tablespoon	lowfat margarine
½ cup	cooked turkey bacon, diced
½ cup	lowfat Swiss cheese, grated
2 tablespoons	fresh chives, chopped
2	green onions, finely chopped

In a medium bowl, beat the eggs with the baking powder and the thyme, whisking until well blended. Place the Steak Plate in the top of the grill and the Baking Pan in the bottom. Set the lever to the back. Set the temperature to Medium to allow the grill to preheat. When the green light goes off, the grill is preheated.

Place the margarine in the grill, close the lid and let the margarine melt for 30 seconds. Pour the eggs into the grill, close the lid and cook for 1½ minutes. Open the grill, place the remaining ingredients on one half of the eggs and use a heat-resistant plastic spatula to fold the other half over to cover. Cook the omelet for 2½ minutes. Check the omelet and continue cooking according to your preference.

Serves 4. ❧

Calories: 173

Total Fat: 12g

Saturated Fat: 4g

% Calories from Fat: 64

Carbohydrates: 2g

Protein: 14g

Cholesterol: 238mg

Sodium: 686mg

Migas

A fabulous traditional Tex-Mex dish, migas (me-gus), can be found on any breakfast menu in the southwest. Serve with salsa, black beans and warmed flour tortillas.

1 cup	liquid egg substitute
½ teaspoon	salt
½ teaspoon	black pepper
1	green onion, chopped
2 tablespoons	Monterey Jack cheese, grated
2 tablespoons	longhorn cheddar cheese, grated
2 tablespoons	jalapeño peppers, chopped
1 tablespoon	lowfat margarine
½ cup	tortilla chips, crumbled

In a medium bowl, whisk together the egg substitute with the salt and pepper. Add the onion, cheeses and the jalapeño peppers and whisk to blend. Place the Steak Plate in the top of the grill and the Baking Pan in the bottom. Set the lever to the back. Set the temperature to Medium to allow the grill to preheat. When the green light goes off, the grill is preheated.

Place the margarine in the grill, close the lid and let the margarine melt for 30 seconds. Pour the migas into the grill, close the lid and cook for 10 seconds. Open the lid and scramble well. Close the lid and cook for an additional 10 seconds. Open the grill and stir in the tortilla chips. Close the lid and cook for 20 seconds or until done according to your preference.

Serves 2. ❧

Calories: 269

Total Fat: 12g

Saturated Fat: 4g

% Calories from Fat: 40

Carbohydrates: 24g

Protein: 18g

Cholesterol: 15mg

Sodium: 1230mg

Red Flannel Hash

This old fashioned, stick-to-your-ribs, recipe is great for breakfast or even a casual dinner.

3 large	red potatoes
½ teaspoon	salt
1 teaspoon	black pepper
3 tablespoons	lowfat margarine
1½ cups	cooked corned beef, diced
1½ cups	cooked beets, diced
¼ cup	white onion, diced
1 tablespoon	fresh parsley, minced

Scrub the potatoes and chop into ¼-inch cubes. Place the Steak Plate in the top of the grill and the Grilling Plate in the bottom. Set the lever to the back. Set the temperature to High to allow the grill to preheat. When the green light goes off, the grill is preheated. Place the potatoes in the grill and dust with salt and pepper. Close the lid and cook for 4 minutes.

Melt the margarine in the microwave oven. In a medium bowl, combine the corned beef, beets, onion, parsley and melted margarine. Use a heat-resistant plastic spatula to transfer the partially cooked potatoes to the bowl with the corned beef mixture, tossing gently to combine. Spread the mixture evenly across the grill, close the lid, and cook for 4 to 5 minutes. Check the hash and continue grilling for 1 to 2 minutes, if necessary.

Serves 4. ❧

Calories: 189

Total Fat: 5g

Saturated Fat: < 1g

% Calories from Fat: 25

Carbohydrates: 16g

Protein: 21g

Cholesterol: 33mg

Sodium: 1129mg

Fresh Home-Baked Biscuits

Spread the warm biscuits with apple butter or honey for a home-baked breakfast treat!

2 cups	all-purpose white flour
2½ teaspoons	baking powder
½ teaspoon	salt
5 tablespoons	lowfat margarine
¾ cup	lowfat milk

In a large bowl, mix the flour, baking powder and salt. Mix the margarine into the flour mixture until it resembles coarse crumbs. Make a well in the middle of the flour mixture and pour in the milk. Gently stir with a fork until the dough forms a mass. Gather the dough with clean hands, form into a ball and place on a floured surface. Knead the dough, pulling the edges to the center and pushing it into itself about 10 times. The dough will feel light and soft, but not sticky. Roll the dough into a circle about ¼-inch thick. Use a 2 to 3-inch round cookie cutter, jar rim or drinking glass rim, to cut out circles as close together as possible.

Place the Steak Plate in the top of grill and the Baking Pan in the bottom. Set the lever to the back. Set the temperature to Medium to allow the grill to preheat. When the green light goes off, the grill is preheated. Place about 6 biscuits in the Baking Pan, 1-inch apart. Close the lid and bake for 6 to 8 minutes, until the biscuits are puffed and golden and the tops are browned. Repeat with the remaining biscuits.

Makes 8 to 12 biscuits. ✍

Calories: 195

Total Fat: 4g

Saturated Fat: 1g

% Calories from Fat: 16

Carbohydrates: 35g

Protein: 5g

Cholesterol: 2mg

Sodium: 471mg

Crispy Hash Browned Potatoes

Browned and crispy on the outside and yummy on the inside—hash browns in 5 minutes! Now everybody's favorite can be a regular part of breakfast, even on busy work day mornings.

2 large	russet potatoes
½ teaspoon	salt
1 teaspoon	black pepper
2 teaspoons	extra-virgin olive oil

Scrub the potatoes and grate on a hand grater. Place the grated potatoes in a wire mesh strainer and gently press to remove all liquid. Dry the potatoes well and toss with salt and pepper.

Place the Steak Plate in the top of the grill and the Grilling Plate in the bottom. Set the lever to the back. Set the temperature to High to allow the grill to preheat. When the green light goes off, the grill is preheated. Place the grated potatoes in the grill and spread to a thickness of ¼-inch. Drizzle the oil over the potatoes and close the lid. Cook for 4 to 5 minutes or until potatoes are tender in the center and crispy browned on the bottom.

Serves 4. ❧

Calories: 70

Total Fat: 2g

Saturated Fat: 0g

% Calories from Fat: 28

Carbohydrates: 10g

Protein: 4g

Cholesterol: 0g

Sodium: 304mg

Cornmeal Muffins

Serve with Red Flannel Hash (p. 20) for a hearty breakfast!

½ cup	all-purpose flour
½ cup	yellow corn meal
1½ tablespoons	sugar
1¼ teaspoons	baking powder
¼ teaspoon	salt
1	egg, lightly beaten
1/3 cup + 2 tablespoons	milk
1½ tablespoons	vegetable oil

In a medium bowl, combine the flour, corn meal, sugar, baking powder and salt, stirring to blend. Add the egg, milk and oil and stir well to blend. The dough will be thick. Place the Steak Plate in the top of the grill and the Baking Pan in the bottom. Set the lever to the back. Set the temperature to Medium to allow the grill to preheat. When the green light goes off, the grill is preheated.

Using a tablespoon, drop the corn muffins in the Baking Pan, one inch apart, and close the lid. Bake for 10 to 12 minutes. Using a heat-resistant plastic spatula, transfer the muffins to a rack and cool slightly. Repeat with the remaining muffin batter.

Makes 16 to 20 muffins. ✺

Calories: 85

Total Fat: 3g

Saturated Fat: <1g

% Calories from Fat: 31

Carbohydrates: 13g

Protein: 2g

Cholesterol: 22mg

Sodium: 120mg

Perfect Morning Waffles

This basic waffle recipe is wonderful as is, or you may want to add pecans and cinnamon to the batter for a special breakfast treat.

¼ to ½ cup	lowfat margarine
1½ cups	all-purpose flour
1 teaspoon	baking powder
⅛ teaspoon	salt
2 tablespoons	sugar
2	eggs
1½ cups	lowfat milk
1 teaspoon	vanilla extract
	nonstick cooking spray

Melt the margarine in the microwave oven. In a medium bowl, combine the dry ingredients. In another medium bowl, whisk the eggs lightly and stir in the milk, vanilla extract and melted margarine. Stir the liquid ingredients into the dry ingredients and mix until just blended. Do not over-blend.

Place the Waffle Plates in the top and bottom of the grill. Set the lever to the back. Set the temperature to High to allow the grill to preheat. When the green light goes off, the grill is preheated. Coat the top and bottom Plates with nonstick cooking spray. Spoon about ⅓-cup of batter onto each side of the bottom Waffle Plate and close the lid. Cook the waffles for 3½ minutes. Check the waffles and continue cooking to a golden brown. Repeat with any remaining batter. Keep warm in the oven or serve immediately with syrup or honey.

Serves 4. ❧

Calories: 298

Total Fat: 7g

Saturated Fat: 2g

% Calories from Fat: 21

Carbohydrates: 47g

Protein: 11g

Cholesterol: 110mg

Sodium: 362mg

Sour Cream Blackberry Waffles

The sweetness of the berries perfectly balances the tart sour cream.

3 tablespoons	lowfat margarine
¾ cup	fresh blackberries, washed and dried
4 tablespoons	sugar, divided
1¾ cups	all-purpose flour
1 teaspoon	baking powder
⅛ teaspoon	salt
2	eggs
¾ cup	lowfat milk
1 cup	nonfat sour cream
	nonstick cooking spray

Melt the margarine in the microwave oven. In a small bowl, combine the berries with 2 tablespoons of sugar. In a medium bowl, combine the flour, baking powder, salt and the remaining 2 tablespoons of sugar. In another medium bowl, whisk the eggs lightly and stir in the milk, sour cream and melted margarine. Stir the liquid ingredients into the dry ingredients and mix until just blended. Do not over-blend. Add the berries and stir once or twice.

Place the Waffle Plates into the top and bottom of the grill. Set the lever to the back. Set the temperature to High to allow the grill to preheat. When the green light goes off, the grill is preheated. Coat the Plates with nonstick cooking spray. Spoon about ⅓-cup of the batter onto each side of the bottom Waffle Plate and close the lid. Cook the waffles for 3½ minutes. Check the waffles and continue cooking until golden brown. Repeat with any remaining batter. Keep warm in the oven or serve immediately with syrup or honey.

Serves 4. ❧

Calories: 407

Total Fat: 6g

Saturated Fat: 2g

% Calories from Fat: 13

Carbohydrates: 72g

Protein: 14g

Cholesterol: 118mg

Sodium: 361mg

Apple Ginger Waffles

Fresh ginger, cinnamon and cloves combine to create an aromatic sensation.

¼ to ½ cup	lowfat margarine
1 cup	all-purpose white flour
1 cup	whole wheat flour
1½ teaspoons	baking powder
2 tablespoons	dark brown sugar
1 teaspoon	ground cinnamon
1 teaspoon	ground cloves
2	eggs
1½ cups	lowfat milk
¼ cup	apple juice
1 tablespoon	fresh ginger, grated
	nonstick cooking spray

Calories: 354

Total Fat: 7g

Saturated Fat: 3g

% Calories from Fat: 19

Carbohydrates: 60g

Protein: 14g

Cholesterol: 110mg

Sodium: 346mg

Melt the margarine in the microwave oven. In a medium bowl, combine the flours, baking powder, sugar, cinnamon and cloves. In another medium bowl, whisk the eggs lightly and stir in the milk, apple juice, ginger and melted margarine. Stir the liquid ingredients into the dry ingredients and mix until just blended. Do not over-blend.

Place the Waffle Plates into the top and bottom of the grill. Set the lever to the back. Set the temperature to High to allow the grill to preheat. When the green light goes off, the grill is preheated. Coat the Plates with nonstick cooking spray. Spoon about ⅓-cup of batter onto each side of the bottom Waffle Plate and close the lid. Cook the waffles for 3½ minutes. Check the waffles and continue cooking until golden brown. Repeat with any remaining batter. Keep warm in the oven or serve immediately with syrup or honey.

Serves 4. ❧

Caper-Dill Waffles with Smoked Salmon Cream Cheese

Like a bagel, but better!

¼ to ½ cup	lowfat margarine
1¾ cups	all-purpose flour
2 teaspoons	baking powder
½ teaspoon	black pepper
2	eggs
¾ cup	lowfat milk
¾ cup	lowfat sour cream
½ cup	red onion, finely diced
3 tablespoons	fresh dill, finely minced
2 tablespoons	capers, drained well
1 cup	nonfat cream cheese, softened
3 ounces	smoked salmon, chopped
1 tablespoon	fresh dill, minced, for garnish
	nonstick cooking spray

Melt the margarine in the microwave oven. In a medium bowl, combine the flour, baking powder and pepper. In another medium bowl, whisk the eggs lightly and stir in the milk, sour cream, onion, dill, capers and melted margarine. Mix the liquid ingredients into the dry ingredients and stir until just blended. Do not over-blend.

To prepare the *Smoked Salmon Cream Cheese*, combine the cream cheese with the smoked salmon in a small bowl, mixing well to blend. Cover and refrigerate until needed.

Place the Waffle Plates into the top and bottom of the grill. Set the lever to the back. Set the temperature to High to allow the grill to preheat. When the green light goes off, the grill is preheated. Coat the Plates with nonstick cooking spray. Spoon about ⅓-cup of the batter onto each side of the bottom Waffle Plate and close the lid. Cook the waffles for 3½ minutes. Check the waffles and continue cooking until golden brown. Repeat with any remaining batter. Serve with the *Smoked Salmon Cream Cheese* and garnish with minced dill.

Serves 4.

Calories: 376

Total Fat: 8g

Saturated Fat: 3g

% Calories from Fat: 19

Carbohydrates: 52g

Protein: 23g

Cholesterol: 114mg

Sodium: 1099mg

27

Oatmeal Cinnamon Raisin Pancakes

Kids will think they are eating cookies for breakfast!

¼ to ½ cup	lowfat margarine
1¼ cups	buttermilk, divided
1 cup	quick-cooking old-fashioned oats (not instant)
1 cup	all-purpose flour
3 tablespoons	dark brown sugar
1½ teaspoons	baking powder
½ teaspoon	baking soda
1 teaspoon	ground cinnamon
1 teaspoon	ground nutmeg
2	eggs
1 teaspoon	vanilla extract
½ cup	raisins
	nonstick cooking spray

Calories: 376

Total Fat: 6g

Saturated Fat: 1g

% Calories from Fat: 14

Carbohydrates: 68g

Protein: 13g

Cholesterol: 111mg

Sodium: 478mg

Melt the margarine in the microwave oven. In a small bowl, combine 1 cup buttermilk with the oats and let stand for 10 minutes. In another small bowl, combine the dry ingredients. In a medium bowl, whisk the eggs lightly and stir in the vanilla extract, melted margarine, oat mixture and the remaining buttermilk. Stir the dry ingredients into the wet ingredients, mixing gently to combine. Add the raisins and stir once or twice.

Place the Waffle Plate in the top of the grill and the Baking Pan in the bottom. Set the lever to the back. Set the temperature to High to allow the grill to preheat. When the green light goes off, the grill is preheated. Coat the grill with nonstick cooking spray. Spoon the batter onto the Baking Pan in ¼-cup measures and close the lid. Cook the pancakes for 3 minutes. Check the pancakes and continue cooking if necessary, until the pancakes are browned and the edges are slightly dry. Keep warm in the oven or serve immediately with syrup or honey. Repeat with the remaining batter.

Serves 4. ❧

Pumpkin Soufflé Pancakes

*The beaten egg whites create a pancake with a fluffy, soufflé-like center.
Fantastic with pure maple syrup!*

3 tablespoons	lowfat margarine
1 cup	all-purpose flour
¼ cup	sugar
1 teaspoon	baking powder
½ teaspoon	ground cinnamon
⅛ teaspoon	ground nutmeg
⅛ teaspoon	ground cloves
⅛ teaspoon	ground allspice
¼ teaspoon	salt
1 cup	lowfat milk
¾ cup	canned pureed pumpkin
4	eggs, separated
1 teaspoon	vanilla extract
	nonstick cooking spray

Melt the margarine in the microwave oven. In a large bowl, combine the dry ingredients. In a medium bowl, whisk together the milk, pumpkin, egg yolks, vanilla extract and melted margarine until well blended. Add the pumpkin mixture to the dry ingredients and stir until smooth. In another medium bowl, beat the egg whites with an electric mixer until stiff, but not dry. Gently fold half of the egg whites into the batter and, once incorporated, fold in the remaining half. The batter will be slightly thick.

Place the Waffle Plate in the top of the grill and the Baking Pan in the bottom. Set the lever to the back. Set the temperature to High to allow the grill to preheat. When the green light goes off, the grill is preheated. Coat the grill with nonstick cooking spray. Spoon the batter onto the Baking Pan in ¼-cup measures and close the lid. Cook the pancakes for 3 minutes. Check the pancakes and continue cooking, if necessary, until the pancakes are browned and the center is puffy and moist. Repeat with any remaining batter. Keep warm in the oven or serve immediately with syrup or honey.

Serves 6.

Calories: 201

Total Fat: 6g

Saturated Fat: 2g

% Calories from Fat: 25

Carbohydrates: 29g

Protein: 8g

Cholesterol: 143mg

Sodium: 356mg

Buttermilk Pancakes

Classic pancakes topped with butter and syrup—without the hassle of the messy cleanup!

2 to 4 tablespoons	lowfat margarine
1 cup	all-purpose flour
½ teaspoon	baking soda
¾ teaspoon	baking powder
½ teaspoon	salt
2 teaspoons	sugar
1	egg
1 cup	buttermilk
	nonstick cooking spray

Calories: 181

Total Fat: 4g

Saturated Fat: <1g

% Calories from Fat: 20

Carbohydrates: 29g

Protein: 7g

Cholesterol: 57mg

Sodium: 692mg

Melt the margarine in the microwave oven. In a medium bowl, combine the flour, baking soda, baking powder, salt and sugar. In another medium bowl, whisk the egg lightly and stir in the buttermilk and melted margarine. Stir the wet ingredients into the dry ingredients and mix until just blended. Do not over-blend.

Place the Waffle Plate in the top of the grill and the Baking Pan in the bottom. Set the lever to the back. Set the temperature to High to allow the grill to preheat. When the green light goes off, the grill is preheated. Coat the grill with nonstick cooking spray. Spoon the batter onto the Baking Pan in ¼-cup measures and close the lid. Cook the pancakes for 3 minutes. Check the pancakes and continue cooking, if necessary, until the pancakes are browned and the center is puffy and moist. Repeat with the remaining batter. Keep warm in the oven or serve immediately with syrup or honey.

Serves 4.

Buckwheat Pancakes with Strawberries & Cream

*The fresh sweetness of the strawberries and cream is fabulous
with the earthy taste of the buckwheat.*

3 to 5 tablespoons	lowfat margarine
½ cup	buckwheat flour
½ cup	all-purpose white flour
1½ teaspoons	baking powder
2 teaspoons	sugar
½ teaspoon	salt
1	egg
1 cup	lowfat milk
2 cups	nonfat whipped topping
1½ cups	fresh strawberries, washed and sliced
	nonstick cooking spray

Melt the margarine in the microwave oven. In a medium bowl, combine the flours, baking powder, sugar and salt. In another medium bowl, whisk the egg lightly and stir in the milk and melted margarine. Stir the wet ingredients into the dry ingredients and mix until just blended. Do not over-blend.

Place the Waffle Plate in the top of the grill and the Baking Pan in the bottom. Set the lever to the back. Set the temperature to High to allow the grill to preheat. When the green light goes off, the grill is preheated. Coat the grill with nonstick cooking spray. Spoon the batter onto the Baking Pan in ¼-cup measures and close the lid. Cook the pancakes for 3 minutes. Check the pancakes and continue cooking, if necessary, until the pancakes are browned and the center is puffy and moist. Repeat with the remaining batter. Serve immediately topped with strawberries and whipped topping.

Serves 4. ❧

Calories: 295

Total Fat: 9g

Saturated Fat: 6g

% Calories from Fat: 28

Carbohydrates: 44g

Protein: 8g

Cholesterol: 56mg

Sodium: 575mg

Breakfast Rice Cakes

A yummy way to use leftover rice, Breakfast Rice Cakes are bound to become a family favorite. Add nuts, dried fruit or your favorite spices. Try adding maple extract with a hint of nutmeg for a fabulous start to a chilly autumn day.

2 to 3 tablespoons	lowfat margarine
2	eggs
¼ cup	sugar
1 teaspoon	vanilla extract
½ teaspoon	ground cinnamon
2 cups	white rice, cooked and cooled
	nonstick cooking spray

Melt the margarine in the microwave oven. In a large bowl, whisk the eggs lightly. Add the sugar, vanilla extract, cinnamon and margarine, mixing well to blend. Add the rice and stir to combine. The mixture should be thick and the rice just coated with the egg mixture.

Place the Waffle Plate in the top of the grill and the Baking Pan in the bottom. Set the lever to the back. Set the temperature to High to allow the grill to preheat. When the green light goes off, the grill is preheated. Coat the grill with nonstick cooking spray. Spoon the batter onto the Baking Pan in ¼-cup measures and close the lid. Cook the rice cakes for 3 minutes. Check the rice cakes and continue cooking, if necessary, until the rice cakes are browned and the center of each is firm. Repeat with the remaining rice cake batter. Keep warm in the oven or serve immediately with butter and jam or syrup.

Serves 4. ❧

Calories: 183

Total Fat: 4g

Saturated Fat: 1g

% Calories from Fat: 21

Carbohydrates: 31g

Protein: 5g

Cholesterol: 106mg

Sodium: 89mg

French Toast with Strawberry Butter

This recipe produces delicious French Toast—without turning! The smooth strawberry butter is easy to make and stores well in the refrigerator, too. Make extra and serve on pancakes or waffles.

2 tablespoons	honey
1 cup	liquid egg substitute
½ cup	lowfat milk
¼ cup	fat-free half and half
1 teaspoon	vanilla extract
½ teaspoon	ground cinnamon
8 slices	dry white, wheat or sourdough bread, challah bread or brioche

Melt the honey in the microwave oven for 15 seconds. In a medium bowl, whisk the egg substitute, milk, half and half, vanilla, cinnamon and honey and pour into a shallow pan. Place the Steak Plate in the top of the grill and the Grilling Plate in the bottom. Set the lever to the back. Set the temperature to High to allow the grill to preheat. When the green light goes off, the grill is preheated.

Dip 2 slices of bread into the mixture and allow to soak for 10 seconds on each side. Place the dipped bread slices on the Grilling Plate and close the lid. Cook for 3 minutes. Check the French toast and continue cooking, if necessary, until golden brown. Repeat with the remaining French toast. Serve immediately topped with a dollop of *Strawberry Butter*.

Serves 4. ❧

Strawberry Butter

4 tablespoons	lowfat margarine, softened
1 tablespoon	strawberry preserves
2 teaspoons	orange zest

In a small bowl, combine the margarine, strawberry preserves and orange zest, mixing well to blend. Refrigerate until ready to use.

Calories: 356

Total Fat: 9g

Saturated Fat: 3g

% Calories from Fat: 22

Carbohydrates: 54g

Protein: 15g

Cholesterol: 44mg

Sodium: 641mg

Pecan Orange Stuffed French Toast

Can French toast really get any better? Yes it can…try it stuffed with Orange-Pecan Cream Cheese. *A scrumptious breakfast treat, perfect for a sunny Sunday morning!*

8 slices	firm bread, sliced 1½-inches thick
1 cup	liquid egg substitute
½ cup	lowfat milk
4 tablespoons	orange juice concentrate
½ teaspoon	ground nutmeg

Calories: 422

Total Fat: 14g

Saturated Fat: 2g

% Calories from Fat: 29

Carbohydrates: 55g

Protein: 23g

Cholesterol: 2mg

Sodium: 814mg

With a sharp knife, cut a 2-inch pocket horizontally into each slice of the bread. Stuff a generous spoonful of the *Orange Pecan Cream Cheese* into the pocket. In a medium bowl, whisk the egg substitute, milk, orange juice concentrate and nutmeg and pour into a shallow pan or dish.

Place the Steak Plate in the top of the grill and the Grilling Plate in the bottom. Set the lever to the back. Set the temperature to High to allow the grill to preheat. When the green light goes off, the grill is preheated. Dip the bread into the egg mixture and allow to soak for 10 seconds on each side. Place 2 of the dipped bread slices on the Grilling Plate and close the lid. Cook for 3 minutes. Check the French toast and continue cooking, if necessary, until golden brown. Repeat with the remaining slices. Keep warm in the oven or serve immediately with butter and syrup.

Serves 4. ❧

Orange Pecan Cream Cheese

8 ounces	nonfat cream cheese, softened
3 tablespoons	orange marmalade
½ cup	pecans, finely chopped

In a small bowl, combine the cream cheese, marmalade and pecans, stirring well to blend. Use as directed above.

Croissant French Toast with Warm Berries

Definitely a splurge! The croissants are dipped in an almond egg batter, grilled to a delightful golden brown and topped with sweetened warm berries. A dusting of powdered sugar finishes this beautiful presentation.

½ cup	fresh raspberries
½ cup	fresh blueberries
½ cup	fresh blackberries
¼ cup	sugar
½ teaspoon	vanilla extract
1 tablespoon	cornstarch
2 tablespoons	cold water
¾ cup	liquid egg substitute
¼ cup	lowfat milk
½ teaspoon	almond extract
4 large	croissants, halved lengthwise
	powdered sugar for dusting

In a small saucepan, combine the berries, sugar and vanilla extract and bring to a boil. Stir and reduce the heat to low. Whisk the cornstarch into the water until dissolved and add to the berries. Simmer for 2 minutes while stirring constantly. In a medium bowl, whisk the egg substitute, milk and almond extract and pour into a shallow pan or dish.

Place the Steak Plate in the top of the grill and the Grilling Plate in the bottom. Set the lever to the back. Set the temperature to High to allow the grill to preheat. When the green light goes off, the grill is preheated. Quickly dip the croissant halves in the batter. Do not soak the croissants because they are soft and may disintegrate. Place the dipped croissants on the Grilling Plate and close the lid. Cook for 3 minutes. Check the French toast and continue cooking, if necessary, until golden brown. To serve, spoon the warm berries into the bottom half of a croissant and cover with the "top half." Dust with the powdered sugar.

Serves 4. ❧

Calories: 348

Total Fat: 12g

Saturated Fat: 7g

% Calories from Fat: 32

Carbohydrates: 49g

Protein: 10g

Cholesterol: 39mg

Sodium: 508mg

Panini, Quesadillas, Sandwiches & More

SIMPLE OR COMPLEX, LARGE OR SMALL, fancy or informal, sandwiches are a perfect choice anytime of the day or evening. Versatile and easily concocted with delicious breads, meats, cheeses, vegetables and a variety of spreads, sandwiches are easy to prepare and even more delicious when heated or grilled.

The recipes in this chapter introduce fresh combinations and take old favorites to new heights. In addition to sandwiches, you'll find panini and quesadillas, as well as dried fruit and fresh vegetables to complement classic sandwich makings. The *Steak & Potato Panini, Eggplant Parmesan Focaccia* and *Crab & Avocado Quesadilla* are among the best choices for fabulous feasts to be grilled or heated in just a few minutes.

If you are searching for a new twist to your favorite sandwiches, try the savory, lowfat spreads and sauces offered in this chapter. Create your own "signature" combinations for spectacular results!

Lemon Garlic Spread

A hearty spread for sandwiches, appetizers or grilled vegetables.

8 cloves	garlic, chopped
2 tablespoons	extra-virgin olive oil
2 tablespoons	fresh lemon juice
¼ teaspoon	salt

Place all the ingredients in a food processor and blend until smooth. Store any unused spread in a covered container in the refrigerator for up to 2 weeks.

Makes about ¼ cup.

Calories: 17

Total Fat: 1g

Saturated Fat: <1g

% Calories from Fat: 72

Carbohydrates: 1g

Protein: <1g

Cholesterol: 0mg

Sodium: 59mg

Tuscan Tomato Spread

A rich spread with an excellent tomato flavor.

½ cup	sun-dried tomatoes, packed in oil, drained
1 clove	garlic, finely minced
½ teaspoon	salt
½ teaspoon	black pepper
¼ cup	lowfat cream cheese

Finely chop the sun-dried tomatoes. In a small glass bowl combine the tomatoes, garlic, salt and pepper, mixing well to blend. Add the cream cheese and blend well. Store any unused spread in a covered container in the refrigerator for up to 2 weeks.

Makes about ¾ cup.

Calories: 47

Total Fat: 4g

Saturated Fat: 2g

% Calories from Fat: 64

Carbohydrates: 3g

Protein: 1g

Cholesterol: 11mg

Sodium: 317mg

Quick Dijonaise Sauce

Perfect for crudités or sandwiches.

½ cup	lowfat mayonnaise
1 tablespoon	Dijon mustard
½ teaspoon	black pepper

In a small bowl, whisk all the ingredients until combined. Store any unused spread in a covered container in the refrigerator for up to 2 weeks.

Makes about ½ cup. ❧

Calories: 56

Total Fat: 2g

Saturated Fat: <1g

% Calories from Fat: 37

Carbohydrates: 9g

Protein: <1g

Cholesterol: <1mg

Sodium: 301mg

Chipotle Mayonnaise

For tacos, tostadas, burritos and more!

½ cup	lowfat mayonnaise
7 ounce	can chipotle chile in adobo sauce, seeded and chopped
1 teaspoon	fresh lime juice

Combine the mayonnaise, chile and lime juice in a food processor and blend until smooth. Store any unused spread in a covered container in the refrigerator for up to 1 week.

Makes about ¾ cup. ❧

Calories: 49

Total Fat: 2g

Saturated Fat: 0g

% Calories from Fat: 39

Carbohydrates: 7g

Protein: 1g

Cholesterol: 0mg

Sodium: 336mg

Duo Olive Tapenade

Create any number of Greek sandwiches starting with this lively spread.

¾ cup	pitted kalamata olives (or any Italian black olives)
¼ cup	pitted Spanish olives (or any green olives)
1 clove	garlic, minced
¼ cup	extra-virgin olive oil
1 tablespoon	fresh Italian flat leaf parsley, minced

Combine the olives, garlic, oil and parsley in a food processor and pulse to combine. The mixture should be almost smooth. Store any unused spread in a covered container in the refrigerator for up to 1 week.

Makes about 1¼ cups. ❧

Calories: 79

Total Fat: 8g

Saturated Fat: 1g

% Calories from Fat: 91

Carbohydrates: 2g

Protein: <1g

Cholesterol: 0mg

Sodium: 198mg

Capresi Panini

Fresh and simple!

2	crusty Italian rolls, sliced in half, horizontally
4 tablespoons	prepared basil pesto
4 slices	fresh buffalo mozzarella cheese (substitute any fresh mozzarella)
2 small	ripe red tomatoes, thinly sliced
1 tablespoon	extra-virgin olive oil

Spread 1 tablespoon of pesto on the cut side of each half of the rolls. Layer the bottom roll half with the mozzarella cheese and tomatoes. Cover with the top half and lightly brush the top of each panini with oil.

Place the Steak Plate in the top of the grill and the Baking Pan in the bottom. Set the lever to the back. Set the temperature to Medium to allow the grill to preheat. When the green light goes off, the grill is preheated. Place the panini in the Baking Pan and close the lid. Cook for 3 to 4 minutes, until the panini are browned and the cheese and tomato are warmed.

Serves 2. ❧

Calories: 530

Total Fat: 33g

Saturated Fat: 8g

% Calories from Fat: 57

Carbohydrates: 32g

Protein: 25g

Cholesterol: 54mg

Sodium: 587mg

Chevre, Fig & Prosciutto Panini

World-class tastes of Italy and France create a luncheon star.

1	seeded soft baguette
4 ounces	chevre (goat cheese)
6 ounces	prosciutto, thinly sliced
2 tablespoons	fig jam
1 teaspoon	extra-virgin olive oil

Slice the baguette in half horizontally. Spread the goat cheese on both of the cut sides of the baguette. On the bottom half of the baguette, layer one half of the prosciutto, spread it with the fig jam and top with remaining prosciutto. Cover with the top half of the baguette. Lightly brush the outside of the baguette with oil.

Place the Steak Plate in the top of the grill and the Baking Pan in the bottom. Set the lever to the back. Set the temperature to Medium to allow the grill to preheat. When the green light goes off, the grill is preheated. Place the panini in the Baking Pan and close the lid. Cook for 3 to 4 minutes, until the outside is browned and the cheese and jam are warmed.

Serves 2. ❧

Calories: 741

Total Fat: 37g

Saturated Fat: 8g

% Calories from Fat: 44

Carbohydrates: 65g

Protein: 42g

Cholesterol: 26mg

Sodium: 2240mg

Steak & Potato Panini

All the trimmings of a steak and potato dinner in a neat, savory package.

1 teaspoon	creamed horseradish
3 tablespoons	lowfat sour cream
4 slices	potato bread, thickly-sliced
8 ounces	beefsteak, cooked medium-rare, thinly sliced
¼ cup	gorgonzola cheese, crumbled
2 tablespoons	fresh chives, minced
1 teaspoon	extra-virgin olive oil

In a small bowl, combine the horseradish and sour cream. Spread ¼ of the mixture over each of the 4 bread slices. Layer 2 bread slices with steak, top with gorgonzola cheese and the minced chives. Place the remaining 2 slices of bread on top and lightly brush the outside of the panini with oil.

Place the Steak Plate in the top of the grill and the Grilling Plate in the bottom. Set the lever to the back. Set the temperature to Medium to allow the grill to preheat. When the green light goes off, the grill is preheated. Place the panini on the Grilling Plate and close the lid. Cook for 3 to 4 minutes, or until the cheese is melted and the panini is hot throughout.

Serves 2. ❧

Calories: 538

Total Fat: 24g

Saturated Fat: 9g

% Calories from Fat: 42

Carbohydrates: 43g

Protein: 33g

Cholesterol: 131mg

Sodium: 703mg

Smoked Turkey, Edam & Orange-Cranberry Panini

A delectable reminder of Thanksgiving!

¼ cup	dried cranberries
2 tablespoons	fresh orange juice
2	Dutch crunch rolls
2 teaspoons	lowfat mayonnaise
8 ounces	smoked turkey, thinly sliced
4 slices	lowfat Edam cheese
4 teaspoons	lowfat margarine

In a small bowl combine the cranberries and orange juice and let stand for 10 minutes, then drain well. Split the rolls in half horizontally and spread the cut sides with mayonnaise. Divide the turkey between the bottom halves of each roll and sprinkle with the cranberries. Top with the cheese. Place the remaining halves on top and lightly spread the top of the panini with margarine.

Place the Steak Plate in the top of the grill and the Baking Pan in the bottom. Set the lever to the back. Set the temperature to Medium to allow the grill to preheat. When the green light goes off, the grill is preheated. Place the panini in the Baking Pan and close the lid. Cook for 3 to 4 minutes until the cheese melts and the panini is warm throughout.

Serves 2. ❧

Calories: 504

Total Fat: 24g

Saturated Fat: 12g

% Calories from Fat: 43

Carbohydrates: 35g

Protein: 37g

Cholesterol: 118mg

Sodium: 1833mg

Eggplant Parmesan Focaccia

A vegetarian offering that is so hearty and satisfying, you won't even miss the meat.

1 small	eggplant
1 teaspoon	salt
1 tablespoon	extra-virgin olive oil
½ teaspoon	black pepper, coarsely ground
1 teaspoon	fresh basil, minced (substitute ¼ teaspoon dried basil)
2 large	rosemary focaccia bread
¼ cup	prepared marinara sauce
2 slices	nonfat mozzarella cheese
2 tablespoons	lowfat Parmesan cheese, shredded
1 teaspoon	extra-virgin olive oil

Calories: 446

Total Fat: 10g

Saturated Fat: <1g

% Calories from Fat: 19

Carbohydrates: 75g

Protein: 19g

Cholesterol: 4mg

Sodium: 969mg

Peel the eggplant and cut into ¼-inch thick slices. Arrange the slices on a double-thickness of paper towels and sprinkle with salt and let stand for 20 minutes. Rinse the eggplant and pat dry. Lightly brush each slice with oil and dust with pepper. Sprinkle the basil over the eggplant slices.

Place the Steak Plate in the top of the grill and the Grilling Plate in the bottom. Set the lever to the back. Set the temperature to Medium to allow the grill to preheat. When the green light goes off, the grill is preheated. Place the eggplant in the Grilling Plate in a single layer and close the lid. Cook for 8 to 10 minutes. Check the eggplant with the tip of a knife and if the eggplant is not tender, continue grilling for 1 to 2 minutes.

Split the focaccia bread in half horizontally. Spread 1 tablespoon of the marinara evenly over 2 focaccia slices and layer with eggplant. Top the eggplant with 1 tablespoon of marinara and top with the cheeses. Cover with the remaining focaccia slices and lightly brush the outside with oil. Place the Steak Plate in the top of the grill and the Baking Pan in the bottom. Set the lever to the back. Set the temperature to Medium to allow the grill to preheat. When the green light goes off, the grill is preheated. Place the panini in the Baking Pan, close the lid, and cook for 3 to 4 minutes, until the cheese is melted and the marinara sauce is hot.

Serves 4. ❧

Cuban Sandwich & Croque Monsieur

This recipe is true to the original. Use Cuban bread if you can find it. If not, a soft French loaf makes a wonderful substitute. A very similar sandwich is the French "Croque Monsieur." To make this classic, simply spread the inside of the bread with Dijon mustard, omit the pork and pickles and use gruyere cheese rather than Swiss.

1 loaf	French bread
4 tablespoons	lowfat margarine, divided
8 ounces	roasted pork, thinly sliced
8 ounces	smoked ham, thinly sliced
4 ounces	lowfat Swiss cheese, sliced
1	dill pickle, thinly sliced

Calories: 436

Total Fat: 17g

Saturated Fat: 6g

% Calories from Fat: 18

Carbohydrates: 30g

Protein: 40g

Cholesterol: 87mg

Sodium: 1274mg

Cut the French loaf in half crosswise and then split in half lengthwise. Spread 2 teaspoons of margarine on the cut side of all 4 slices. Layer half of the pork, ham, cheese and pickles on the bottom half of each roll and cover with roll top. Spread the outside of each sandwich with 2 teaspoons of margarine. Cut each sandwich in half.

Place the Steak Plate in the top of the grill and the Grilling Plate in the bottom. Set the lever to the back. Set the temperature to High to allow the grill to preheat. When the green light goes off, the grill is preheated. Place 2 sandwichs in the grill and close the lid. Cook for 2 to 3 minutes until the cheese is melted. Repeat with the remaining 2 sandwiches.

Serves 4. ❧

Hot Sausage & Peppers Sandwich

A favorite at the "Feast of San Gennaro," in New York's Little Italy.

2	grilled lowfat Italian sausage, or any lowfat sausage, split lengthwise (see Basic Cooking Guide for grilling instructions, p. 114)
4 pieces	sourdough bread, thickly-sliced
4 ounce	jar roasted red peppers
2 slices	provolone cheese
1 teaspoon	extra-virgin olive oil

Place 2 grilled sausage halves, cut side up, on 2 bread slices. Lay the roasted red pepper over the sausage and top with slices of provolone cheese. Place the remaining 2 bread slices on top and lightly brush the outside of each with oil.

Place the Steak Plate in the top of the grill and the Grilling Plate in the bottom. Set the lever to the back. Set the temperature to High to allow the grill to preheat. When the green light goes off, the grill is preheated. Place the sandwiches on the Grilling Plate and close the lid. Cook for 2 to 3 minutes, until the cheese is melted.

Serves 2. ❧

Calories: 459

Total Fat: 28g

Saturated Fat: 10g

% Calories from Fat: 54

Carbohydrates: 34g

Protein: 19g

Cholesterol: 50mg

Sodium: 1108mg

45

Albacore Tuna Melt

A classic made the easy way. Serve with Greek Chicken Orzo Salad (p. 52).

3 tablespoons	lowfat mayonnaise
2 teaspoons	fresh lemon juice
1 teaspoon	black pepper
1 teaspoon	capers, drained
6 ounce	can albacore tuna, packed in water, drained well
4 slices	sourdough bread, thickly-sliced
4 teaspoons	lowfat margarine

Calories: 324

Total Fat: 7g

Saturated Fat: 1g

% Calories from Fat: 20

Carbohydrates: 38g

Protein: 28g

Cholesterol: 38mg

Sodium: 1124mg

In a small bowl, combine the mayonnaise, lemon juice, pepper, capers and tuna, mixing well to blend. Spread ½ of the tuna mixture over 2 slices of bread and cover the tuna with the remaining slices. Lightly spread the outside of the bread with margarine.

Place the Steak Plate in the top of the grill and the Baking Pan in the bottom. Set the lever to the back. Set the temperature to Medium to allow the grill to preheat. When the green light goes off, the grill is preheated. Place the tuna melt in the Baking Pan and close the lid. Cook for 3 to 4 minutes, until the tuna sandwiches are hot and golden brown.

Serves 2. ❧

Greek Olive & Lamb in Pita

All the great flavors of Greece are combined in a handy pita bread.
This is sure to become a favorite!

3 tablespoons	Duo Olive Tapenade *(p. 39)*
2 tablespoons	lowfat feta cheese, crumbled
2	pita breads, large
8 ounces	lean lamb tenderloin, cooked, thinly sliced
1 teaspoon	extra-virgin olive oil
1 cup	romaine lettuce, shredded
1 small	ripe tomato, chopped

In a small bowl combine the *Duo Olive Tapenade* and crumbled feta. Split each pita bread open halfway through to form a pocket. Spread half of the tapenade in each pita and top with sliced lamb. Lightly brush the outside of the pita with oil.

Place the Steak Plate in the top of the grill and the Baking Pan in the bottom. Set the lever to the back. Set the temperature to Medium to allow the grill to preheat. When the green light goes off, the grill is preheated. Place the pita in the Baking Pan and close the lid. Cook for 2 to 3 minutes until the outside is lightly browned and the lamb and tapenade are warmed. Transfer the sandwiches to individual serving plates and carefully stuff with shredded lettuce and tomatoes.

Serves 2. ❧

Calories: 443

Total Fat: 18g

Saturated Fat: 6g

% Calories from
Fat: 37

Carbohydrates: 38g

Protein: 32g

Cholesterol: 95mg

Sodium: 670mg

Grilled Vegetable Calzone

Lowfat and healthy, but packed with flavor.

2	zucchini, thinly sliced
½ small	red onion, thinly sliced
1 small	Portobello mushroom, thinly sliced
2 cloves	garlic, finely minced
1 teaspoon	black pepper
½ loaf	frozen bread dough, thawed
4 tablespoons	Tuscan Tomato Spread (p.37)
1 cup	nonfat mozzarella cheese, shredded
1 teaspoon	extra-virgin olive oil
	nonstick olive oil cooking spray

Calories: 485

Total Fat: 8g

Saturated Fat: 2g

% Calories from Fat: 14

Carbohydrates: 77g

Protein: 35g

Cholesterol 19mg

Sodium: 1604mg

Place the Steak Plate in the top of the grill and the Baking Pan in the bottom. Set the lever to the back. Set the temperature to Medium to allow the grill to preheat. When the green light goes off, the grill is preheated. Spray the top and bottom plates with nonstick cooking spray and place the vegetables in the grill in a single layer. Top with the minced garlic and dust with pepper. Close the lid. Cook the vegetables for 5 minutes. Check the vegetables with the tip of a knife and continue grilling for 1 to 2 minutes if they are not yet tender. Remove the vegetables and set aside.

Divide the dough in half. On a lightly floured board, roll out each half into an 8-inch circle, about 1/8-inch thick. Divide the grilled vegetables evenly between the two calzone, placing them on one half of each dough circle, leaving one half of the dough without a topping.

Spoon the *Tuscan Tomato Spread* over the vegetables and top with the cheese. Fold the unfilled half circle of dough over the toppings and press the edges together to form a tight seal. Brush the outside of each calzone lightly with oil. Place the Steak Plate in the top of the grill and the Baking Pan in the bottom. Set the lever to the back. Set the temperature to Medium to allow the grill to preheat. When the green light goes off, the grill is preheated. Place one calzone in the grill and close the lid. Cook for 7 to 8 minutes. Check the calzone and continue grilling, if necessary. Repeat with the remaining calzone.

Serves 2. ❧

Crab & Avocado Quesadilla

The mango and green chilies combine to add amazing flavor. Great for lunch
or as an appetizer served with a dipping salsa.

8 ounces	fresh lump crab meat or (substitute 6 ounces canned lump crab meat)
4 ounce	can green chiles, chopped
½ cup	fresh mango, chopped
2 tablespoons	nonfat sour cream
½ cup	reduced-fat Monterey Jack cheese, shredded
4	nonfat flour tortillas
1	ripe avocado, thinly sliced

In a small bowl, combine the crab, chilies, mango, sour cream and cheese. Spread one-fourth of the mixture on one half of each tortilla, top with one-fourth of the avocado slices and fold the other half of the tortilla over the filling.

Place the Steak Plate in the top of the grill and the Baking Pan in the bottom. Set the lever to the back. Set the temperature to High to allow the grill to preheat. When the green light goes off, the grill is preheated. Place the quesadillas in the Baking Pan and close the lid. Cook for 2 to 3 minutes until the cheese is melted and the tortillas are soft and slightly browned.

Serves 2.

Calories: 481

Total Fat: 21g

Saturated Fat: 6g

% Calories from Fat: 38

Carbohydrates: 45g

Protein: 31g

Cholesterol: 18mg

Sodium: 1259mg

49

Chicken & Gruyere Quesadilla

European flavors wrapped in a Mexican tortilla create an international sensation!

4 large	spinach flour tortillas
4 teaspoons	Quick Dijonnaise Sauce (p. 38)
2	boneless, skinless chicken breasts, cooked, thinly sliced
4	crimini mushrooms, very thinly sliced
1 tablespoon	fresh tarragon, chopped
½ teaspoon	salt
1 teaspoon	black pepper
4 slices	gruyere cheese

Calories: 296

Total Fat: 11g

Saturated Fat: 6g

% Calories from Fat: 17

Carbohydrates: 24g

Protein: 52

Cholesterol: 52mg

Sodium: 545mg

Spread each tortilla with 1 teaspoon of the *Quick Dijonnaise Sauce* and arrange one-fourth of the chicken slices on one half of each tortilla. Top each with one-fourth of the sliced mushrooms, a sprinkling of chopped tarragon, salt, pepper and one slice of cheese. Fold each tortilla over the filled half.

Place the Steak Plate in the top of the grill and the Baking Pan in the bottom. Set the lever to the back. Set the temperature to High to allow the grill to preheat. When the green light goes off, the grill is preheated. Place the quesadillas in the Baking Pan and close the lid. Cook for 2 to 3 minutes until the cheese is melted and the tortillas are soft and slightly browned.

Serves 4.

4

Salads & Sides

*G*RILLED VEGETABLES, CRISP SALADS AND TENDER FRUIT make any meal special. The recipes in this chapter are suitable for a luncheon or light dinner entrée in addition to complementing grilled steaks, chops, chicken or fish. Whether you choose to grill vegetables or fruit or prepare them with other ingredients in a side dish, you will find that the George Foreman® The Next Grilleration™ G5 is the perfect partner for grilling or cooking complementary side dishes.

Vegetables are packed with vitamins and nutrients that are easily lost when overcooked in boiling water. Grilling vegetables, such as eggplant, squash, onions, potatoes and carrots, releases and seals in their natural juices, creating tender-crisp packets bursting with fresh flavor—and the nutrients are preserved. For best results, cut vegetables and fruit to a uniform size for even cooking. Tossing vegetables with fresh herbs, spices and citrus juices offers added zest without the calories or fat. Serve *Lemon-Honey Glazed Carrots* as a delightful side dish to *Stuffed Flank Steak* or add grilled bell peppers or mushrooms to cooked pasta, sandwiches or omelets.

Greek Chicken Orzo Salad

A beautifully colorful salad with healthy fresh flavors makes a wonderful lunch or dinner entrée or salad.

2 halves	boneless, skinless chicken breast
½ teaspoon	ground cinnamon
1 teaspoon	ground oregano, divided
½ teaspoon	salt
1 teaspoon	black pepper
8 ounces	orzo, cooked and cooled
1	ripe tomato, chopped
1 small	green bell pepper, chopped
6	green onions, chopped
¼ cup	fresh parsley, chopped
¼ cup	extra-virgin olive oil
1½ tablespoons	red wine vinegar
3 tablespoons	nonfat mayonnaise

Calories: 272

Total Fat: 11g

Saturated Fat: <1g

% Calories from Fat: 35

Carbohydrates: 31g

Protein: 14g

Cholesterol: 14mg

Sodium: 278mg

Dust the chicken breasts with the cinnamon, ½-teaspoon oregano, salt and pepper. Place the Steak Plate in the top of the grill and the Grilling Plate in the bottom. Set the lever to the front. Set the temperature to High to allow the grill to preheat. When the green light goes off, the grill is preheated. Place the chicken on the Grilling Plate and close the lid. Cook for 5 minutes. Check the chicken with the tip of a knife and continue grilling until no pink remains and the internal temperature of the chicken reaches 180°F. Cool the chicken and cut into small pieces. In a serving bowl, combine the orzo, tomato, green pepper, green onions, parsley and chicken. In a small bowl, whisk together the oil, vinegar, mayonnaise, and ½-teaspoon oregano and pour over the salad, tossing lightly to combine. Adjust the seasonings with salt and pepper.

Serves 6. ❧

Grilled & Chilled Seafood Salad

This rich-flavored, yet lowfat salad is cool and satisfying on a hot summer day.

12 medium	sea scallops
8 ounces	halibut, cut into 1-inch pieces
12 small	shrimp, cleaned and deveined
3 tablespoons	fresh lemon juice, divided
1½ teaspoons	black pepper, divided
1	yellow bell pepper, thinly sliced
1	green bell pepper, thinly sliced
1	red bell pepper, thinly sliced
3 tablespoons	fresh parsley, minced
¼ cup	extra-virgin olive oil
2 tablespoons	tarragon vinegar
½ teaspoon	salt

In a small bowl, toss the seafood with 1 tablespoon of lemon juice and 1 teaspoon of black pepper. Place the Steak Plate in the top of the grill and the Grilling Plate in the bottom. Set the lever to the back. Set the temperature to Medium to allow the grill to preheat. When the green light goes off, the grill is preheated. Place the scallops and halibut on the Grilling Plate and close the lid. Cook for 4 minutes. Remove the scallops with a heat-resistant plastic spatula. Add the shrimp to the halibut and cook for an additional 2 minutes. Check the fish with the tip of a knife and continue grilling the halibut, if necessary.

Cool the seafood. In a large serving bowl, combine the sliced peppers, parsley and cooled seafood. In a small bowl, whisk together the oil, vinegar, remaining lemon juice, salt and remaining pepper until well-blended. Pour over the salad, tossing lightly to combine. Cover the salad with plastic wrap and refrigerate for 1 hour before serving.

Serves 4.

Calories: 159

Total Fat: 3g

Saturated Fat: <1g

% Calories from Fat: 17

Carbohydrates: 9g

Protein: 24g

Cholesterol: 60mg

Sodium: 424mg

Grilled Beef with Root Vegetables
& Orange Vinaigrette

Deep colors and rich flavors blend to create a hearty and refreshing chilled salad entrée.

½ pound	lean beef
2 tablespoons	low sodium soy sauce
2 tablespoons	pomegranate juice
1¼ teaspoons	black pepper, divided
1 large	celery root
2 large	carrots
6 medium	beets, cooked (substitute 8.5 oz can cooked beets)
1	shallot, minced
2 tablespoons	fresh orange juice
1 tablespoon	white wine vinegar
¼ cup	extra-virgin olive oil
¼ teaspoon	salt
1 tablespoon	orange zest (optional garnish)

Calories: 362

Total Fat: 27g

Saturated Fat: 5g

% Calories from Fat: 65

Carbohydrates: 19g

Protein: 14g

Cholesterol: 40mg

Sodium: 581mg

Remove any visible fat from the beef and cut into very thin slices. In a resealable plastic bag, combine the soy sauce, pomegranate juice and 1 teaspoon of the pepper. Add the beef slices and seal the bag tightly. Turn and squeeze the bag to coat the beef with the marinade. Refrigerate for 1 hour.

Place the Steak Plate in the top of the grill and the Grilling Plate in the bottom. Set the lever to the front. Set the temperature to High to allow the grill to preheat. When the green light goes off, the grill is preheated. Place the beef strips on the Grilling Plate and close the lid. Cook for 2 minutes. Check the beef with the tip of a knife and continue grilling, if desired.

Cool the beef. Peel the celery root and carrots. Cut the celery root, carrots and beets into matchstick pieces and place in a large bowl with the cooled beef. In a small bowl, whisk together the shallot, orange juice, white wine vinegar, oil, salt and the remaining pepper. Pour the dressing over the salad and garnish with the orange zest. Cover tightly and refrigerate for 1 hour.

Serves 4. ❧

Grilled Garlic & Potato Salad

Grilled garlic adds incredible flavor to this salad; you will not even miss the extra fat.

4 small	red potatoes
1 teaspoon	extra-virgin olive oil
1 teaspoon	dried basil
1 teaspoon	dried oregano
1 teaspoon	dried thyme
10 whole cloves	garlic, peeled
½ teaspoon	salt
1 teaspoon	black pepper
4 tablespoons	nonfat mayonnaise
1 tablespoon	nonfat sour cream
2 tablespoons	capers
½ teaspoon	Dijon mustard
1 teaspoon	red wine vinegar
1 teaspoon	water
1 small	green onion, sliced
¼ cup	fresh parsley, minced
2	hard-cooked eggs, grated

Scrub the potatoes and cut into ¼-inch thick slices. In a small bowl combine the oil, basil, oregano, thyme, garlic cloves and potato slices and toss to coat. Place the Steak Plate in the top of the grill and the Grilling Plate in the bottom. Set the lever to the back. Set the temperature to High to allow the grill to preheat. When the green light goes off, the grill is preheated. Place one-half of the potato mixture on the Grilling Plate in a single layer, close the lid, and cook for 7 minutes. Check and continue cooking for 1 to 2 minutes, or until tender. Remove to a platter to cool. Repeat with the remaining half.

Repeat with the remaining potatoes and garlic until all are cooked. Peel the cooked garlic. In a small bowl, mash the grilled garlic and add the salt, pepper, mayonnaise, sour cream, capers, mustard, vinegar and water. In a large bowl, combine the onion, parsley, eggs, and potatoes. Add the dressing and stir gently to combine. Refrigerate for 1 hour to allow the flavors to blend. Adjust the seasonings with salt and pepper.

Serves 6. ❧

Calories: 86

Total Fat: 3g

Saturated Fat: <1g

% Calories from Fat: 27

Carbohydrates: 11g

Protein: 5g

Cholesterol: 71mg

Sodium: 395mg

Yukon Ranch Potatoes

*A savory aroma fills the air while grilling this delicious blend of peppers and potatoes,
turning your kitchen into a mountain-top chuckwagon.*

4 medium	Yukon Gold potatoes
½ small	red bell pepper, diced
½ small	green bell pepper, diced
½ small	yellow onion, diced
2 strips	uncooked lean bacon, diced
3 teaspoons	seasoned salt
1 tablespoon	fresh parsley, minced

Scrub the potatoes and cut into ¼ inch-thick cubes. Place in a medium bowl along with the peppers, onion, bacon, seasoned salt and parsley and toss well to combine.

Place the Steak Plate in the top of the grill and the Grilling Plate in the bottom. Set the lever to the back. Set the temperature to High to allow the grill to preheat. When the green light goes off, the grill is preheated. Place the potato mixture on the Grilling Plate in a single layer and close the lid. Grill for 4 minutes. Use a heat-resistant plastic spatula to turn and stir the potatoes and cook for an additional 4 to 5 minutes. Check the potatoes and continue cooking until tender and slightly browned.

Serves 4. ❧

Calories: 78

Total Fat: 1g

Saturated Fat: <1g

% Calories from
Fat: 14

Carbohydrates: 13g

Protein: 6g

Cholesterol: 5mg

Sodium: 1061mg

Yukon Ranch Potatoes p. 56

Simply Scrambled Eggs p. 15 and Buttermilk Pancakes p. 30

Cornmeal Muffins p. 23

Pacific Rim Salmon Steaks p. 88

Beef Medallions with Tomatillo Pesto *p. 69*

Grilled Vegetable Calzone   p. 48

Maple Orange Sauce p. 101 and Kasbah Spice Rub p. 105

Chocolate Chip Cookies p.113

Lemon-Honey Glazed Carrots

An effortless, yet elegant glaze adds a hint of spice to sweet grilled carrots.

4	carrots, peeled and cut into ½-inch thick slices
1 teaspoon	extra-virgin olive oil
2 tablespoons	lowfat margarine
1 small	shallot, sliced
¼ cup	fresh lemon juice
2 tablespoons	clover honey
⅛ teaspoon	ground cardamom

Place the Steak Plate in the top of the grill and the Grilling Plate in the bottom. Set the lever to the back. Set the temperature to Medium to allow the grill to preheat. When the green light goes off, the grill is preheated. Place the carrots on the Grilling Plate in a single layer and drizzle with oil. Close the lid and cook for 7 minutes. Check the carrots and continue cooking for 1 to 2 minutes, or until the carrots are tender-crisp.

In a small saucepan over medium-low heat, melt the margarine. Add the shallot and sauté for 2 minutes or until softened. Stir in the lemon juice, honey and cardamom, constantly mixing to blend and heat through. Add the grilled carrots and toss to coat. Serve while hot.

Serves 4. ᑫ❧

Calories: 85

Total Fat: 3g

Saturated Fat: <1g

% Calories from Fat: 27

Carbohydrates: 16g

Protein: <1g

Cholesterol: 0mg

Sodium: 77mg

Grilled Japanese Vegetables with Wasabi Butter

The earthy flavors of the eggplant contrasts with the buttery softness of the kabocha to create a delightful vegetable medley. You'll find wasabi in the specialty ethnic food aisle of your grocery store.

2	Japanese eggplant
¼ pound	kabocha (substitute any winter squash)
3 tablespoons	lowfat margarine
½ teaspoon	salt
½ teaspoon	black pepper
½ teaspoon	wasabi
¾ teaspoon	ground ginger
½ teaspoon	salt
1 tablespoon	fresh lime juice
1 teaspoon	extra-virgin olive oil

Calories: 102

Total Fat: 4g

Saturated Fat: <1g

% Calories from Fat: 31

Carbohydrates: 17g

Protein: 3g

Cholesterol: 0mg

Sodium: 672m

Clean the eggplant and slice into ¼-inch thick slices. Clean the kabocha, remove the seeds and woody fibers and cut into small ¼-inch thick cubes. Melt the margarine in the microwave and add the salt, pepper, wasabi, ginger, salt and lime juice, stirring until well-blended.

Place the Steak Plate in the top of the grill and the Grilling Plate in the bottom. Set the lever to the back. Set the temperature to Medium to allow the grill to preheat. When the green light goes off, the grill is preheated. Brush the eggplant with oil and place the eggplant and squash on the Grilling Plate in a single layer. Close the lid. Grill for 4 minutes, drizzle the eggplant and squash with wasabi butter, and continue grilling for an additional 4 to 5 minutes. Check the vegetables with the tip of a knife and continue grilling for 1 to 2 minutes, or until the vegetables are tender. Use a heat-resistant plastic spatula to transfer the vegetables to a serving plate, mounding squash on top of eggplant slices. Drizzle with any remaining wasabi butter.

Serves 4. ✑

Grilled Garnet Yams with Fruit & Spiced Butter

Great with grilled ham to complete a special Sunday family dinner.

¼ cup	lowfat margarine
½ teaspoon	ground cinnamon
½ teaspoon	ground nutmeg
2	garnet yams
1	sweet orange
½ cup	fresh pineapple, cut into small chunks (substitute ½ cup canned pineapple chunks, drained)

In a small bowl, melt the margarine in the microwave oven and combine with the cinnamon and nutmeg. Peel the yams and cut into ¼-inch thick slices. Peel the orange and cut into thin slices. Place the Steak Plate in the top of the grill and the Grilling Plate in the bottom. Set the lever to the back. Set the temperature to High to allow the grill to preheat. When the green light goes off, the grill is preheated. Place the yam slices on the Grilling Plate and close the lid. Cook for 5 minutes. Place the orange slices on the yams and arrange the pineapple chunks around the sides. Drizzle the spiced butter over all and continue cooking for 2 to 3 minutes. As the yams cook, the spiced butter will run into the drip tray. Use a heat-resistant plastic spatula to transfer the yams to a serving platter. Top with the grilled pineapple and drizzle with melted butter from the drip tray.

Serves 4.

Calories: 301

Total Fat: 4g

Saturated Fat: 1g

% Calories from Fat: 10

Carbohydrates: 65g

Protein: 4g

Cholesterol: 0mg

Sodium: 130mg

Beef, Lamb & Pork

AN EXCELLENT STEAK IS A WORK OF ART, especially when grilled to perfection in the George Foreman® The Next Grilleration™ G5. Top the steak with crumbled blue cheese and serve it with a crisp green salad—it becomes a meal fit for a king. But, even a king needs to watch his fat intake! Luckily, there are numerous lean cuts of beef, pork and lamb that are rich in flavor and lower in calories. Beef tenderloin, beef flank steak and lean lamb chops are all great, lower-fat choices and you'll find recipes for each in this chapter.

The unique design of the George Foreman® The Next Grilleration™ G5 allows the fat to drip away from meat as it grills, producing succulent grilled meat without the fat. The Steak Plate creates pleasing "char marks" in true steakhouse fashion as the meat grills. If the meat is of an uneven thickness, portions of the steak may grill more quickly than others, so check the meat and re-position it if necessary. Keep in mind that the meat will continue to cook slightly after it has been removed from the grill so remove the meat from the grill while it is still a bit undercooked.

Beef Medallions with Tomatillo Pesto

The fresh pesto perfectly complements the rich flavor of the beef.

6	fresh tomatillos, quartered
¼ cup	fresh cilantro
¼ cup	fresh Italian flat leaf parsley
¼ cup	pine nuts
2 cloves	garlic, roughly chopped
1 tablespoon	extra-virgin olive oil
½ teaspoon	salt
1 teaspoon	black pepper
1½ pounds	lean beef tenderloin
1 clove	garlic, peeled and split lengthwise
	salt and pepper for dusting

Place the tomatillos, cilantro, parsley, pine nuts, garlic, olive oil, salt and pepper into a food processor and blend until smooth. For the best results, refrigerate for 1 hour.

Cut the beef into 1-inch thick slices across the grain, rub with the split garlic clove and dust with salt and pepper.

Place the Steak Plate in the top of the grill and the Grilling Plate in the bottom. Set the lever to the front. Set the temperature to High to allow the grill to preheat. When the green light goes off, the grill is preheated. Place the beef medallions on the Grilling Plate and close the lid. Cook for 4 to 5 minutes. Check the beef and continue grilling, if necessary, or according to your preference. Serve the beef medallions topped with the tomatillo pesto.

Serves 4. ❧

Calories: 378

Total Fat: 30g

Saturated Fat: 11g

% Calories from Fat: 72

Carbohydrates: 4g

Protein: 23g

Cholesterol: 79mg

Sodium: 252mg

Stuffed Flank Steak

The savory stuffing cooks inside the steak, absorbing all the juices and rich flavors.
For a classic meal that always satisfies, serve with Yukon Ranch Potatoes (p. 56)
and fresh steamed asparagus.

2 pounds	lean beef flank steak
¼ cup	fresh basil, finely minced
¼ cup	crimini mushrooms, chopped
¼ cup	sun-dried tomatoes, packed in oil, drained and chopped
⅓ pound	lowfat turkey sausage, casing removed

Remove any visible fat from the steak. With a sharp knife, cut a slit sideways into the steak without cutting completely through the meat, to form a large pocket. In a medium bowl, combine the basil, mushrooms, sun-dried tomatoes and sausage. Mix well and stuff into the pocket of the steak in a 1-inch layer. Press the sides of the steak together to close or secure with a toothpick, if desired. Gently pat the top of the steak to evenly spread out the stuffing.

Place the Steak Plate in the top of the grill and the Grilling Plate in the bottom. Set the lever to the back. Set the temperature to High to allow the grill to preheat. When the green light goes off, the grill is preheated. Place the flank steak on the Grilling Plate and close the lid. Cook for 6 to 7 minutes. Check the beef and sausage stuffing and continue grilling according to your preference. To serve, cut the steak across the grain into thick slices.

Serves 4. ❧

Calories: 319

Total Fat: 19g

Saturated Fat: 7g

% Calories from Fat: 53

Carbohydrates: 2g

Protein: 35g

Cholesterol: 96mg

Sodium: 342mg

Tenderloin Steaks with Grilled Mushrooms & Blue Cheese

A lower fat version of the traditional bacon wrapped fillet.

4 ounces	fresh mushrooms, sliced (substitute 4 ounce can sliced mushrooms, drained)
1 strip	turkey bacon, cut into 4 pieces
4	4 ounce beef tenderloin steaks
	salt and black pepper
4 teaspoons	blue cheese, crumbled (substitute gorgonzola cheese)

Place the Steak Plate in the top of the grill and the Grilling Plate in the bottom. Set the lever to the front. Set the temperature to High to allow the grill to preheat. When the green light goes off, the grill is preheated.

Place the mushrooms on the Grilling Plate and top with the bacon. Close the lid and cook on High for 8 minutes. Check the mushrooms and bacon and continue cooking until the bacon is crisp and mushrooms are browned around the edges. Remove with a heat-resistant plastic spatula, remove the bacon and reserve for another use. Keep the mushrooms warm.

Remove any visible fat from the steaks and dust with salt and pepper to taste. Place the filets in the grill and close the lid. Cook for 4 minutes. Check the steaks and continue grilling according to your preference. To serve, place each steak on an individual plate and top with 1 teaspoon of the crumbled cheese and grilled mushrooms.

Serves 4.

Calories: 334

Total Fat: 26g

Saturated Fat: 11g

% Calories from Fat: 71

Carbohydrates: 1g

Protein: 22g

Cholesterol: 84mg

Sodium: 136mg

Korean Barbeque

Traditionally grilled at the table, the barbeque can be rolled into lettuce leaves and served with green onions, chopped garlic and Asian chili sauce.

1½ pounds	ribeye steak
¼ cup	low sodium soy sauce
1½ tablespoons	rice wine vinegar
1 tablespoon	sesame seeds
1 tablespoon	fresh ginger, grated
1 tablespoon	dark brown sugar
1 tablespoon	sesame oil
1 tablespoon	honey
2 cloves	garlic, chopped
2	green onions, chopped
¼ teaspoon	crushed red pepper

Calories: 372

Total Fat: 28g

Saturated Fat: 10g

% Calories from Fat: 68

Carbohydrates: 8g

Protein: 21g

Cholesterol: 77mg

Sodium: 403mg

Remove any visible fat from the steak. Cut the steak into very thin slices and place in a flat glass pan. In a small bowl, combine the remaining ingredients and pour over the steak, turning the steak a few times to evenly coat the beef. Cover tightly with plastic wrap and refrigerate for 1 hour or up to 8 hours.

Place the Steak Plate in the top of the grill and the Grilling Plate in the bottom. Set the lever to the front. Set the temperature to High to allow the grill to preheat. When the green light goes off, the grill is preheated. Place the steak strips on the Grilling Plate and discard the marinade. Close the lid. Cook for 5 minutes. Check the steak and continue grilling according to your preference.

Serves 6. ❧

Caribbean Lamb with Mint Yogurt Sauce

Serve these delicious lamb patties as a main entrée with savory couscous and a green salad with a spicy vinaigrette. These lamb patties are also excellent when stuffed into grilled pita bread and topped with the yogurt sauce.

1 pound	ground lamb
2 tablespoons	fresh parsley, finely minced
2 tablespoons	red onion, finely minced
1 clove	garlic, finely minced
1 tablespoon	ground allspice
½ teaspoon	chili powder

In a medium bowl, combine the lamb with the parsley, onion, garlic, allspice and chili powder. Shape the lamb mixture into 4 patties.

Place the Steak Plate in the top of the grill and the Grilling Plate in the bottom. Set the lever to the front. Set the temperature to Medium to allow the grill to preheat. When the green light goes off, the grill is preheated. Place the lamb patties on the Grilling Plate and close the lid. Grill for 6 minutes. Check the lamb with the tip of a knife and continue cooking for 1 to 2 minutes, or according to your preference. Serve with *Mint Yogurt Sauce*.

Serves 4. ❧

Mint Yogurt Sauce

½ cup	plain nonfat yogurt
½ cup	nonfat sour cream
2 teaspoons	fresh lemon juice
1 tablespoon	clover honey
2 tablespoons	fresh mint leaves, finely minced

In a small bowl combine the yogurt, sour cream, lemon juice, honey and mint leaves, mixing well to blend. Cover and refrigerate until use.

Calories: 395

Total Fat: 27g

Saturated Fat: 12g

% Calories from Fat: 62

Carbohydrates: 15g

Protein: 22g

Cholesterol: 89mg

Sodium: 117mg:

Lamb Chops Stuffed with Greek Gremolata

The classic combination of mint and lamb is enhanced with traditional Greek flavors of lemon and almonds. Lovely for an Easter or springtime dinner.

¼ cup	fresh mint leaves
¼ cup	fresh parsley
1 tablespoon	roasted almonds
1 clove	garlic, crushed
1 tablespoon	fresh lemon juice
1 tablespoon	extra-virgin olive oil
4	lamb rib chops, 1½-inches thick
½ teaspoon	salt
½ teaspoon	black pepper

Place the mint, parsley, almonds, garlic, lemon juice and oil in a food processor and pulse until roughly chopped. Remove all visible fat from the chops and place the chops on a clean cutting surface. With the tip of a sharp knife, cut a slit sideways (horizontally) into each chop to create a pocket. Stuff one-fourth of the gremolata into each chop and press the edges of the pocket to close.

Place the Steak Plate in the top of grill and the Grilling Plate in the bottom. Set the lever to the front. Set the temperature to Medium to allow the grill to preheat. When the green light goes off, the grill is preheated. Place the chops on the Grilling Plate, dust with salt and pepper and close the lid. Cook for 6 minutes. Check the lamb with the tip of a knife and continue cooking for 1 to 2 minutes, or according to your preference.

Serves 4. ❧

Calories: 343

Total Fat: 30g

Saturated Fat: 11g

% Calories from Fat: 79

Carbohydrates: 2g

Protein: 16g

Cholesterol: 70mg

Sodium: 347mg

Island Jerked Pork with Lime Crème Fraîche

In Jamaica, allspice (pimento) branches are placed in the barbeque grill to enhance the flavor of the jerked meat. The jerked meat is then traditionally chopped into pieces and served with a hard-dough bread.

1½ pounds	country-style boneless pork ribs
¼ cup	jarred pimento
3 tablespoons	light brown sugar
3 cloves	garlic, chopped
1	Serrano chile, seeded and chopped
2 teaspoons	ground allspice
2 tablespoons	low sodium soy sauce
1 teaspoon	salt
1 teaspoon	black pepper
½ cup	crème fraîche or lowfat sour cream
1 teaspoon	lime zest
1 tablespoon	fresh lime juice

Remove all visible fat from the pork and place in a resealable plastic bag. Place the pimento, brown sugar, garlic, chile, allspice, soy sauce, salt and pepper into a food processor and process until well-blended. Pour the jerk sauce into the bag with the pork and tightly seal. Gently squeeze and turn the bag to coat all sides of the pork. Refrigerate for up to 8 hours. In a small bowl, whisk the crème fraîche or sour cream with the lime zest and juice and set aside.

Place the Steak Plate in the top of the grill and the Grilling Plate in the bottom. Set the lever to the front. Set the temperature to Medium to allow the grill to preheat. When the green light goes off, the grill is preheated. Place the pork ribs on the Grilling Plate and discard the marinade. Close the lid. Cook the ribs for 7 to 9 minutes. Check the ribs with the tip of a knife and continue grilling for 1 to 2 minutes, if necessary. Serve on individual plates with a drizzle of lime crème fraîche.

Serves 4.

Calories: 449

Total Fat: 23g

Saturated Fat: 8g

% Calories from Fat: 48

Carbohydrates: 20g

Protein: 38g

Cholesterol: 107mg

Sodium: 937mg

Pork Tenderloin with Quick Raspberry Sauce

The sauce creates an elegant dish worthy of dinner party status.

4	6 ounce pork tenderloins
	salt and black pepper, to taste
1 tablespoon	raspberry vinegar
3 tablespoons	orange marmalade
3 tablespoons	seedless raspberry jam
⅛ teaspoon	ground cardamom

Remove any visible fat from the pork and dust lightly with salt and pepper. In a small glass bowl, combine the vinegar, marmalade, jam and cardamom and heat in the microwave oven for 30 seconds. Set aside.

Place the Steak Plate in the top of the grill and the Grilling Plate in the bottom. Set the lever to the front. Set the temperature to Medium to allow the grill to preheat. When the green light goes off, the grill is preheated. Place the tenderloins on the Grilling Plate and close the lid. Cook for 2 minutes. Spoon a little sauce over each tenderloin and continue cooking for 3 minutes. Check the tenderloin with the tip of a knife and continue grilling for 1 to 2 minutes, if necessary.

To serve, thinly slice across the grain of the meat, arrange the pork slices on individual plates and drizzle with any remaining sauce.

Serves 4. ❧

Calories: 309

Total Fat: 9g

Saturated Fat: 3g

% Calories from
Fat: 28

Carbohydrates: 19g

Protein: 35g

Cholesterol: 112mg

Sodium: 92mg

Dijon Mushroom Stuffed Pork Chops

Serve with grilled asparagus and garlic mashed potatoes for a satisfying dinner.

¼ pound	button mushrooms, cleaned and chopped
1	shallot, finely minced
4 teaspoons	extra-virgin olive oil, divided
	salt and black pepper, to taste
2 tablespoons	Dijon mustard
¾ cup	soft bread crumbs
2 teaspoons	dried tarragon
4	6 ounce boneless pork loin chops, 1½-inch thick

Place the Steak Plate in the top of the grill and the Grilling Plate in the bottom. Set the lever to the front. Set the temperature to Medium to allow the grill to preheat. When the green light goes off, the grill is preheated. Place the mushrooms and shallots on the Grilling Plate, drizzle with 1 teaspoon of oil and dust with salt and pepper. Close the lid. Cook for 4 minutes. Using a heat-resistant plastic spatula, transfer the mushrooms and shallots to a small bowl. Cool slightly and add the mustard, bread crumbs, tarragon and 3 teaspoons of the oil, mixing well with your finger tips to combine. The mixture should adhere slightly. Moisten with a few drops of water, if needed.

Remove any visible fat from the pork. With a sharp knife, create a pocket by cutting a slit sideways almost completely through each chop. Stuff a generous amount of the Dijon mixture into each pocket and press a spoonful onto the top of the chop to create a thin crust.

Place the Steak Plate in the top of the grill and the Grilling Plate in the bottom. Set the lever to the front. Set the temperature to Medium to allow the grill to preheat. When the green light goes off, the grill is preheated. Place the pork chops on the Grilling Plate and close the lid. Cook for 4 to 5 minutes. Check the pork chops with the tip of a knife and continue grilling according to your preference.

Serves 4.

Calories: 533

Total Fat: 34g

Saturated Fat: 7g

% Calories from Fat: 58

Carbohydrates: 17g

Protein: 39g

Cholesterol: 99mg

Sodium: 292mg

Santa Fe Pork Ribs

Boneless ribs and a spicy rub create a quick, but spectacular barbeque.
Great served with fresh corn on the cob. Add a salad of spring greens, pine nuts,
drained black beans and avocado tossed with a creamy cilantro dressing.

1½ pounds	country-style boneless pork ribs
4 tablespoons	ground New Mexican red chile
4 tablespoons	dark brown sugar
6 tablespoons	canned tomato paste
2 teaspoons	salt
2 teaspoons	ground cumin
1 teaspoon	ground dried oregano

Remove any visible fat from the ribs. Score the ribs with a knife to prevent the meat from curling as it grills. In a small bowl, combine the remaining ingredients and let stand for 10 minutes to allow the flavors to blend. Generously rub the sauce into all sides of the pork ribs and let the ribs marinate for 1 hour.

Place the Steak Plate in the top of grill and the Grilling Plate in the bottom. Set the lever to the front. Set the temperature to Medium to allow the grill to preheat. When the green light goes off, the grill is preheated. Place the ribs on the Grilling Plate and close the lid. Cook for 7 to 9 minutes. Check the ribs with the tip of a knife and continue grilling an additional 1 to 2 minutes, if necessary.

Serves 4. ❧

Calories: 307

Total Fat: 16g

Saturated Fat: 5g

% Calories from Fat: 48

Carbohydrates: 15g

Protein: 25g

Cholesterol: 68mg

Sodium: 889mg

Chapter six

Dinner Entrées

Chicken, Seafood & Vegetarian Dishes

RICH IN FLAVOR AND PROTEIN, YET LOW IN FAT, poultry is a great choice for any meal. Chicken and turkey are versatile and can be paired with a world of flavors and spices to create a multitude of delectable tastes at the table. In the pages of this chapter, you'll find such delights as *Crispy Baked Chicken, Chicken Piccata* and *Simple Lemon Thyme Turkey*.

When grilling poultry, always check for doneness in order to avoid bacteria. Chicken and turkey should be cooked until no pink remains, juices run clear and a meat thermometer reads 180ºF. When defrosting or marinating poultry, always keep the poultry in the refrigerator and use hot, soapy water to wash all surfaces that have come in contact with raw poultry.

Fish and seafood from fresh water and the ocean are a gift of healthy flavor. Packed with essential nutrients, fish is a beneficial choice for everyone and offers a wide diversity of flavors and textures—from a very firm swordfish steak to delicious and tender brook trout. Grilled fish is fantastic when paired with an appropriate marinade or sauce. For delicious and easy meals, try *Herb-Crusted Salmon with*

Yellow Tomato Relish, Dijon Lemon Oysters with Angel Hair Pasta and *Pacific Rim Salmon Steaks*. Experiment with flavors you like and add to fresh fish and shellfish as they become available during the year.

When meat is not on the menu, grilling up a vegetarian main course is an easy task to accomplish. Use the George Foreman® The Next Grilleration™ G5 to beautifully grill such delights as *Grilled Polenta with Vegetable Marinara* and *Stuffed Chile Rellenos*. Satisfy your craving for hearty goodness by grilling Portobello mushrooms, adding a splash of balsamic vinegar and dusting with fresh herbs. Vegetarian main courses are easily made delicious and healthful—just use your imagination!

Grilled Chicken Mole

Mole (mo-lay) is a balanced Mexican blending of sweet and spicy that fluctuates by region.
Slice the chicken and serve with warmed tortillas.

2 tablespoons	ground New Mexican red chile (substitute any ground red chile)
1 tablespoon	instant powdered espresso
1 tablespoon	cocoa powder
2 teaspoons	powdered sugar
2 teaspoons	toasted almonds, finely ground
1 teaspoon	salt
½ teaspoon	ground coriander
¼ teaspoon	ground cinnamon
¼ teaspoon	ground cloves
4 halves	boneless, skinless chicken breasts

Combine all the ingredients except the chicken on a large plate and mix thoroughly. Press each chicken breast into the spices, coating all sides. Place the Steak Plate in the top of the grill and the Grilling Plate in the bottom. Set the lever to the front. Set the temperature to Medium to allow the grill to preheat. When the green light goes off, the grill is preheated. Place the chicken on the Grilling Plate and close the lid. Cook for 6 minutes. Discard the marinade. Check the chicken with the tip of a knife and continue grilling until no pink remains and the internal temperature of the meat reaches 180°F.

Serves 4.

Calories: 112

Total Fat: 2g

Saturated Fat: <1g

% Calories from Fat: 19

Carbohydrates: 5g

Protein: 18g

Cholesterol: 41mg

Sodium: 667mg

Crispy Baked Chicken

Golden fried chicken without the fat!

4 halves	boneless, skinless chicken breasts
1	egg, beaten
1 cup	buttermilk
3 dashes	Tabasco® Sauce
¾ cup	yellow cornmeal
¼ cup	all-purpose flour
2 teaspoons	ground paprika
½ teaspoon	salt
1 teaspoon	black pepper
	nonstick cooking spray

Calories: 235

Total Fat: 3g

Saturated Fat: <1g

% Calories from Fat: 13

Carbohydrates: 28g

Protein: 23g

Cholesterol: 94mg

Sodium: 428mg

Place the chicken breasts between two pieces of plastic wrap and pound to a thickness of ½-inch. In a flat glass pan, beat the egg and add the buttermilk and Tabasco® sauce. On a large plate, combine the cornmeal, flour, paprika, salt and pepper. Dip the chicken in the buttermilk mixture, then into the cornmeal mixture, turning to coat all sides and pressing the cornmeal mixture firmly into each chicken breast. Shake the excess cornmeal mixture from the chicken and place on a wire rack. Let the chicken set on the rack for 20 to 30 minutes.

Place the Steak Plate in the top of the grill and the Baking Pan in the bottom. Set the lever to the back. Set the temperature to High to allow the grill to preheat. When the green light goes off, the grill is preheated. Spray each chicken breast with nonstick cooking spray, place the chicken in the Baking Pan and close the lid. Cook for 4 minutes. Check the chicken with the tip of a knife and continue grilling until no pink remains and the internal temperature of the chicken reaches 180°F. The chicken is crisp when done.

Serves 4. ❧

Artichoke Stuffed Chicken

Serve with angel hair pasta tossed with olive oil, fresh garlic, lemon juice and Romano cheese.

14 ounce	can artichoke hearts, packed in water, drained
2 tablespoons	fresh lemon juice
1 teaspoon	lemon zest
2 tablespoons	Romano cheese, grated
1 clove	garlic, chopped
2 tablespoons	extra-virgin olive oil
4 halves	boneless, skinless chicken breasts
½ teaspoon	salt
1 teaspoon	black pepper

Place the artichoke hearts, lemon juice, lemon zest, cheese, garlic and olive oil in a food processor and process until blended. Place the chicken on a clean cutting surface. With the tip of a sharp knife, slit each breast horizontally without cutting all the way through to create a pocket. Stuff one-fourth of the stuffing into each chicken breast and press the edges to close. Dust the chicken with salt and pepper.

Place the Steak Plate in the top of the grill and the Grilling Plate in the bottom. Set the lever to the back. Set the temperature to Medium to allow the grill to preheat. When the green light goes off, the grill is preheated. Place the chicken breasts on the Grilling Plate and close the lid. Cook for 6 minutes. Check the chicken with the tip of a knife and continue grilling until no pink remains and the internal temperature of the meat reaches 180ºF. Scoop up any stuffing that spilled out during cooking and serve with the chicken.

Serves 4. ❧

Calories: 201

Total Fat: 9g

Saturated Fat: <1g

% Calories from Fat: 42

Carbohydrates: 9g

Protein: 19g

Cholesterol: 44mg

Sodium: 799mg

Paprika Game Hens
with Moroccan Couscous

Ask your butcher to butterfly the game hens to save time. This meal is especially easy when completed with a chilled vegetable salad, and warm dinner rolls with butter.

3 tablespoons	Hungarian paprika
½ teaspoon	salt
1 teaspoon	black pepper
2 halves	Cornish game hen, flattened (ask your butcher to do this for you)
1½ cups	chicken broth
1 teaspoon	ground cumin
½ teaspoon	ground nutmeg
2 tablespoons	golden raisins
1 tablespoon	pine nuts, toasted
1 cup	dried couscous
1 teaspoon	fresh cilantro, finely minced

Calories: 293

Total Fat: 4g

Saturated Fat: <1g

% Calories from Fat: 13

Carbohydrates: 41g

Protein: 21g

Cholesterol: 55mg

Sodium: 404mg

Mix the paprika with the salt and pepper, rub into the game hen and refrigerate for 30 minutes or up to 8 hours. In a small saucepan, heat the chicken broth, cumin, nutmeg, raisins and pine nuts to a boil, stirring to combine. Remove from the heat. Add the couscous, stirring once or twice, cover the pan and let stand for 10 minutes.

Place the Steak Plate in the top of the grill and the Grilling Plate in the bottom. Set the lever to the front. Set the temperature to Medium to allow the grill to preheat. When the green light goes off, the grill is preheated. Place the game hen halves on the Grilling Plate and close the lid. Cook for 8 to 10 minutes. Check the game hen with the tip of a knife and continue grilling until no pink remains and the internal temperature of the game hens reaches 180ºF. (note: the skin may be removed before serving for a lower fat meal). To serve, fluff the couscous with a fork, add the cilantro and place on a serving platter. Arrange the game hen halves on top and serve immediately.

Serves 2. ❧

Simple Lemon Thyme Turkey

Serve with steamed broccoli and a green salad for a delicious lowfat meal.

1 pound	boneless, skinless turkey breast
¼ cup	extra-virgin olive oil
¼ cup	fresh lemon juice
1 tablespoon	lemon zest
2 cloves	garlic, finely minced
4 tablespoons	fresh thyme, finely minced
1 teaspoon	salt
1 teaspoon	black pepper

Slice the turkey breast horizontally across the grain into 1-inch thick slices and place in a flat glass pan. In a small bowl, whisk together the oil, lemon juice, lemon zest, garlic, thyme, salt and pepper. Pour the marinade over the turkey, turning a few times to coat. Cover tightly with plastic wrap and refrigerate for 1 to 4 hours, turning once.

Place the Steak Plate in the top of the grill and the Grilling Plate in the bottom. Set the lever to the back. Set the temperature to Medium to allow the grill to preheat. When the green light goes off, the grill is preheated. Place the turkey slices on the Grilling Plate and close the lid. Cook for 5 minutes. Discard the marinade. Check the turkey with the tip of a knife and continue grilling until no pink remains and the internal temperature reaches 180°F.

Serves 4.

Calories: 309

Total Fat: 22g

Saturated Fat: 2g

% Calories from Fat: 64

Carbohydrates: 3g

Protein: 25g

Cholesterol: 74mg

Sodium: 649mg

Chicken Piccata

For a quick midweek meal, serve with fresh pasta, which cooks much faster than dried. Check the refrigerated case at your grocery store for a wide variety of fresh pasta shapes and sizes.

4 halves	boneless, skinless chicken breasts
¼ cup	all-purpose flour
1 teaspoon	salt
1 teaspoon	lemon pepper
4 teaspoons	extra-virgin olive oil
3 tablespoons	lowfat margarine
1 tablespoon	extra-virgin olive oil
3 tablespoons	fresh flat leaf parsley, finely minced
3 tablespoons	fresh lemon juice
¼ cup	chicken broth
3 tablespoons	capers
1	lemon, wedged

Calories: 204

Total Fat: 12g

Saturated Fat: 1g

% Calories from Fat: 51

Carbohydrates: 8g

Protein: 18g

Cholesterol: 41mg

Sodium: 973mg

Place the chicken breast halves between two pieces of plastic wrap and pound to a thickness of ½-inch. In a flat glass pan, mix the flour, salt and lemon pepper and press each chicken breast into the flour mixture, turning to coat all sides.

Place the Steak Plate in the top of the grill and the Baking Pan in the bottom. Set the lever to the back. Set the temperature to High to allow the grill to preheat. When the green light goes off, the grill is preheated. Drizzle 2 teaspoons of oil in the Baking Pan. Shake the excess flour from the chicken and place the chicken in the Baking Pan. Drizzle the chicken with the remaining 2 teaspoons of oil and close the lid. Cook for 4 minutes. Check the chicken with the tip of a knife and continue grilling until no pink remains and the internal temperature of the chicken reaches 180ºF.

In a small saucepan, melt the margarine with 1 tablespoon olive oil and add the parsley, lemon juice, chicken broth and capers and simmer over medium-low heat for 3 minutes. Serve the chicken on individual plates topped with a generous spoonful of sauce and garnish with a lemon wedge.

Serves 4. ❧

Sun-dried Tomato Chicken & Zucchini with Penne

*The basil and sun-dried tomato pesto adds a deep richness to the tomato sauce.
The zucchini are brushed with the sun-dried tomato oil before grilling to create a pasta dish
your family and friends will absolutely love.*

1 cup	fresh basil
1 cup	sun-dried tomatoes, packed in oil, coarsely chopped, oil reserved
2 cloves	garlic, crushed
1/3 cup	pine nuts
1 teaspoon	black pepper
2 tablespoons	extra-virgin olive oil
4 halves	boneless, skinless chicken breast
1	24 ounce can Italian plum tomatoes in puree
2 small	zucchini, cut into 1/2-inch thick slices, lengthwise
10 ounces	penne pasta, cooked
1/2 cup	fresh Parmesan cheese, grated

Calories: 572

Total Fat: 19g

Saturated Fat: 3g

% Calories from Fat: 30

Carbohydrates: 63g

Protein: 39g

Cholesterol: 49mg

Sodium: 546mg

Place the basil, tomato, garlic, pine nuts and pepper into a food processor and blend until smooth. With the motor running, drizzle in the olive oil. Cut the chicken breasts into 1-inch strips, place in a medium bowl and toss with 1/4 of the pesto, leaving the remaining pesto in the food processor. Cover the chicken tightly with plastic wrap and refrigerate for 1 hour. Add the can of tomatoes to the pesto in the food processor and blend until smooth. Transfer the sauce to a small saucepan and simmer over low heat for 4 minutes.

Place the Steak Plate in the top of the grill and the Grilling Plate in the bottom. Set the lever to the front. Set the temperature to High to allow the grill to preheat. When the green light goes off, the grill is preheated. Brush the zucchini slices with the reserved sun-dried tomato oil. Place the chicken strips and zucchini on the Grilling Plate and close the lid. Cook for 4 minutes. Check the chicken with the tip of a knife and continue grilling until no pink remains and the internal temperature of the chicken reaches 180ºF. To serve, place the pasta on a serving platter, pour the tomato sauce over the pasta, arrange the chicken and zucchini on top and garnish with grated cheese.

Serves 4.

Pacific Rim Salmon Steaks

The marinated shallots are grilled on top of the salmon, forming a delicious crispy crust.

2	6 ounce salmon steaks
1	shallot, thinly sliced
1¼ teaspoons	fresh ginger, grated
1 teaspoon	Dijon mustard
1 teaspoon	toasted sesame oil
⅓ cup	low sodium soy sauce
1½ tablespoons	maple syrup
½ teaspoon	Asian chile garlic sauce

Place the salmon in a flat glass pan. In a small bowl, combine the remaining ingredients and pour over the salmon steaks. Cover the pan tightly with plastic wrap and refrigerate for 1 to 2 hours.

Place the Steak Plate in the top of the grill and the Grilling Plate in the bottom. Set the lever to the front. Set the temperature to Medium to allow the grill to preheat. When the green light goes off, the grill is preheated. Place the salmon steaks on the Grilling Plate and top with a tablespoon of marinade, scooping up as many sliced shallots as possible and spooning them over each steak. Discard any remaining marinade or, if desired, you may boil the marinade for 5 minutes (to kill any bacteria) and use the hot marinade as a wonderful sauce. Close the lid. Cook the salmon for 7 minutes. Check the fish with the tip of a knife and continue grilling for 1 to 2 minutes, if necessary.

Serves 4.

Calories: 208

Total Fat: 10g

Saturated Fat: 2g

% Calories from Fat: 45

Carbohydrates: 9g

Protein: 19g

Cholesterol: 56mg

Sodium: 769mg

Grilled Swordfish Fajitas

Try these fantastic swordfish fajitas for a change of pace as a lighter alternative to beef or chicken.

1	white onion, thinly sliced into half rings
1 small	red bell pepper, seeded and thinly sliced
1 small	green bell pepper, seeded and thinly sliced
2 cloves	garlic, minced
2 tablespoons	extra-virgin olive oil
½ teaspoon	salt
1 teaspoon	black pepper
2	6 ounce swordfish steaks
1	fresh lime, cut in half
4	flour tortillas, heated
	prepared guacamole
	lowfat sour cream

In a medium bowl, toss the onion, bell peppers and garlic with the oil, salt and pepper. Place the Steak Plate in the top of the grill and the Grilling Plate in the bottom. Set the lever to the front. Set the temperature to Medium to allow the grill to preheat. When the green light goes off, the grill is preheated. Place the swordfish and vegetables on the Grilling Plate and squeeze the lime over all. Close the lid. Grill for 8 minutes. Check the fish with the tip of a knife and continue grilling for 1 to 2 minutes, if necessary. To serve, slice the swordfish and divide between the tortillas. Top with the grilled onions and peppers and garnish with guacamole and sour cream.

Serves 2. ✄

Calories: 512

Total Fat: 21g

Saturated Fat: 2g

% Calories from Fat: 37

Carbohydrates: 42g

Protein: 40g

Cholesterol: 66mg

Sodium: 809mg

Herb-Crusted Salmon with Yellow Tomato Relish

Perfect for a summer feast when luscious tomatoes are abundant and so full of flavor. The fresh relish is a delicious complement to the herb-crusted salmon filets.

2	yellow tomatoes, seeded and diced
1 tablespoon	fresh basil, finely minced
1 small	shallot, finely minced
1 clove	garlic, finely minced
1 tablespoon	extra-virgin olive oil
½ teaspoon	salt
1 teaspoon	black pepper
4 tablespoons	lowfat margarine
½ cup	dry bread crumbs
½ teaspoon	salt
1 teaspoon	black pepper
2 teaspoons	dried parsley
2 teaspoons	dried basil
1 teaspoon	dried oregano
4	6 ounce salmon fillets
	nonstick cooking spray

Calories: 434

Total Fat: 25g

Saturated Fat: 5g

% Calories from Fat: 53

Carbohydrates: 13g

Protein: 37g

Cholesterol: 112mg

Sodium: 901mg

In a small glass bowl, combine the tomatoes, basil, shallot, garlic, oil, salt and 1 teaspoon of pepper. Cover and allow to stand, un-refrigerated, for 1 to 4 hours. In a small bowl, combine the margarine, bread crumbs, salt, pepper and dried herbs, mixing until thoroughly blended but still crumbly. Spread equal amounts of the herb-crumb mixture onto the top of each fillet and flatten to form a crust.

Place the Steak Plate in the top of grill and the Grilling Plate in the bottom. Set the lever to the front. Set the temperature to Medium to allow the grill to preheat. When the green light goes off, the grill is preheated. Spray the bottom and top Plates with cooking spray. Place the fillets on the Grilling Plate and close the lid. Cook for 7 minutes. Check the fish with the tip of a knife and continue grilling for 1 to 2 minutes, if necessary. Serve the grilled salmon topped with the yellow tomato sauce.

Serves 4. ❧

Maryland Crab Cakes

Serve with tarter sauce and lemon wedges. Your guests will never suspect these are a lowfat alternative to pan fried crab cakes.

8 ounces	fresh lump crab meat (substitute 6 ounce can lump crab meat)
3 tablespoons	celery, minced
2 teaspoons	fresh parsley, finely minced
2 teaspoons	fresh lemon juice
¼ teaspoon	Worcestershire sauce
¼ cup	lowfat mayonnaise
½ teaspoon	Dijon mustard
1	egg yolk, slightly beaten
2 teaspoons	seafood seasoning
¼ teaspoon	black pepper
⅛ teaspoon	baking powder
¼ cup	bread crumbs
¾ cup	corn meal
1 to 3 tablespoons	canola oil, divided

In a medium bowl, combine all the ingredients except the corn meal and canola oil, mixing well, but gently to combine. Form the mixture into 8 small patties, about ½-inch thick. Pour the corn meal onto a plate and dredge each crab cake through the corn meal, turning to coat all sides. Place on a baking sheet and cover with plastic wrap and refrigerate 1 hour, or up to 8 hours.

Place the Steak Plate in the top of the grill and the Baking Pan in the bottom. Set the lever to the back. Set the temperature to High to allow the grill to preheat. When the green light goes off, the grill is preheated. Drizzle 1 tablespoon of canola oil in the Baking Pan. Place the crab cakes on the grill, but do not crowd. Close the lid. Cook in multiple batches, if necessary. Cook for 4 minutes. Check the fish with the tip of a knife and continue grilling for 1 to 2 minutes until golden brown.

Serves 4. ∽

Calories: 237

Total Fat: 8g

Saturated Fat: <1g

% Calories from Fat: 28

Carbohydrates: 28g

Protein: 16g

Cholesterol: 93mg

Sodium: 428mg

Dijon Lemon Oysters with Angel Hair Pasta

A simple sauce and fabulous grilled oysters create an outstanding seashore entrée.
Serve with a chilled vegetable salad and crusty French bread.

3 tablespoons	fresh lemon juice
1 teaspoon	lemon zest
2 teaspoons	Dijon mustard
¼ cup+2 tablespoons	extra-virgin olive oil
¼ teaspoon	salt
½ teaspoon	ground black pepper
2 cloves	garlic, finely minced
3 tablespoons	fresh parsley, chopped, divided
12	fresh oysters
6 ounces	dried angel hair pasta, cooked al dente

Calories: 699

Total Fat: 23g

Saturated Fat: 2g

% Calories from Fat: 30

Carbohydrates: 82g

Protein: 40g

Cholesterol: 150mg

Sodium: 641mg

In a small bowl or lidded jar, combine the lemon juice, lemon zest, mustard, oil, salt, pepper, garlic and 2 tablespoons of parsley, whisking or shaking to blend well. Wash the oysters and individually wrap in damp paper towels. In batches of 3 at a time, microwave the towel-wrapped oysters on high for 15 seconds, until the oysters open slightly. Times will vary with microwaves, so check the oysters and continue cooking if needed. Remove the top oyster shell by inserting and twisting the tip of a table knife. Extract the oyster meat and transfer to a small bowl, discarding the shells. Spoon 3 tablespoons of lemon-mustard sauce over the oysters, reserving the remaining sauce, and let stand for 5 minutes.

Place the Steak Plate in the top of the grill and the Baking Pan in the bottom. Set the lever to the back. Set the temperature to Medium to allow the grill to preheat. When the green light goes off, the grill is preheated. Place the oysters in the Baking Pan and discard the marinade. Close the lid. Grill the oysters for 30 seconds to 1 minute. Check the oysters and continue grilling if needed.

To serve, place the hot pasta in a serving bowl and toss with the reserved lemon-mustard sauce. Divide the pasta between 2 individual plates, top with the grilled oysters and the remaining tablespoon of chopped parsley.

Serves 2.

Stuffed Chile Rellenos

Usually deep fried, this lower fat version will become a family favorite.

1 cup	brown rice, cooked
¼ teaspoon	ground nutmeg
½ teaspoon	salt
¼ teaspoon	ground cumin
½ teaspoon	red chili powder
½ small	white onion, minced
2 cloves	garlic, minced
¼ cup	currants
¼ cup	toasted pine nuts
¼ cup	fresh cilantro, minced
1 cup	Monterey Jack cheese, grated
4	fresh poblano chiles, peeled, seeds and stem removed (substitute 4 canned peeled whole green chiles)
2	eggs
1 cup	all-purpose flour
¼ cup	yellow corn meal
2 tablespoons	canola oil, divided

Calories: 451

Total Fat: 21g

Saturated Fat: 6g

% Calories from Fat: 41

Carbohydrates: 49g

Protein: 18g

Cholesterol: 126mg

Sodium: 665mg

In a medium bowl, combine the rice, nutmeg, salt, cumin, chile powder, onion, garlic, currants, pine nuts, cilantro and cheese. Cut a short lengthwise slit in each chile and stuff each with one-fourth of the rice mixture. Close the slit and secure with a toothpick. In a shallow pan, whisk the eggs. Mix the flour and corn meal together in a shallow pan. Dip the chiles in the egg, and then carefully roll in the flour. Carefully shake to remove as much excess flour as possible.

Place the Steak Plate in the top of the grill and the Baking Pan in the bottom. Set the lever to the back. Set the temperature to High to allow the grill to preheat. When the green light goes off, the grill is preheated. Drizzle 1 tablespoon of oil in the Baking Pan. Place the chiles in the Baking Pan and drizzle the remaining oil over the chiles. Close the lid. Cook for 7 minutes. Check the chiles and continue grilling for 1 to 2 minutes, until the cheese is melted and the chilies are golden brown. Serve with garnishes such as salsa, lowfat sour cream or lowfat guacamole.

Serves 4.

Grilled Teriyaki Tofu

Serve with brown rice and steamed vegetables for a tasty healthy, meatless dinner.

14 ounces	firm tofu
¼ cup	low-sodium soy sauce
1 teaspoon	fresh ginger, grated
2 cloves	garlic, minced
1 teaspoon	sesame oil
2 tablespoons	rice wine vinegar

Wrap the tofu in paper towels and place in a shallow pan. Position a plate on top of the tofu and put a heavy object on top of the plate. The weight will remove the excess liquid from the tofu. Allow to stand for at least 30 minutes. Slice the tofu lengthways into 4 slices and place in a shallow glass pan.

In a small bowl combine the soy sauce, ginger, garlic, oil and vinegar. Pour the marinade over the tofu, cover tightly and refrigerate for 1 hour or overnight, turning once or twice to coat.

Place the Steak Plate in the top of the grill and the Grilling Plate in the bottom. Set the lever to the back. Set the temperature to High to allow the grill to preheat. When the green light goes off, the grill is preheated. Place the tofu on the Grilling Plate, discard the marinade and close the lid. Cook for 6 to 7 minutes. Check the tofu and continue grilling for 1 to 2 minutes or until the tofu is thoroughly heated through and the outside is browned.

Serves 4. ∿

Calories: 89

Total Fat: 4g

Saturated Fat: 0g

% Calories from Fat: 40

Carbohydrates: 5g

Protein: 9g

Cholesterol: 0mg

Sodium: 541mg

Spinach Stuffed Eggplant

Healthy and vibrant with beautiful colors and the rich flavors of the Mediterranean.

2 medium	eggplants
½ teaspoon	salt
5 ounces	frozen spinach, chopped, thawed and drained
½ cup	nonfat ricotta cheese
½ cup	lowfat feta cheese, crumbled
2 cloves	garlic, chopped
1 teaspoon	dried oregano
½ teaspoon	nutmeg
1 teaspoon	salt
1 teaspoon	black pepper
1 teaspoon	balsamic vinegar
1 tablespoon	extra-virgin olive oil
10 ounces	spaghetti, cooked, hot
1 cup	prepared marinara sauce, heated
½ cup	Romano cheese, grated

Calories: 540

Total Fat: 16g

Saturated Fat: 6g

% Calories from Fat: 26

Carbohydrates: 76g

Protein: 27g

Cholesterol: 32mg

Sodium: 1339mg

Wash the eggplants and slice lengthwise into 1½-inch thick slices. Arrange on a double-thickness of paper towels and sprinkle with salt. Let stand for 10 minutes. Rinse the eggplant and pat dry. With the tip of a sharp knife, cut a slit in each eggplant horizontally, without cutting all the way through, to create a large pocket.

In a medium bowl, thoroughly combine the spinach, ricotta cheese, feta cheese, garlic, oregano, nutmeg, salt, pepper and vinegar. Stuff each eggplant with the spinach stuffing and press the edges together to close the pocket. Brush the eggplant lightly with oil and dust with salt and pepper.

Place the Steak Plate in the top of the grill and the Grilling Plate in the bottom. Set the lever to the back. Set the temperature to Medium to allow the grill to preheat. When the green light goes off, the grill is preheated. Place the eggplant on the Grilling Plate in a single layer and close the lid. Cook for 9 to 10 minutes. Check the eggplant with the tip of a knife. Continue grilling until the eggplant is tender To serve, place the pasta on a serving platter, cover with heated sauce and arrange the stuffed eggplant on top. Garnish with Romano cheese.

Serves 4. ❧

Grilled Polenta with Vegetable Marinara

A superb pairing of fresh tastes and textures that is low in fat and high in flavor.

24 ounce	tube of prepared plain polenta
1 teaspoon	extra-virgin olive oil
½	yellow onion, diced
2 tablespoons	extra-virgin olive oil
1 small	zucchini, diced
2 cloves	garlic, minced
¼ pound	fresh mushrooms, trimmed and sliced
½ teaspoon	salt
1 teaspoon	black pepper
¾ cup	vegetable broth
3 tablespoons	tomato paste
14½ ounce	can diced tomatoes
2 tablespoons	fresh basil, chopped

Calories: 517

Total Fat: 14g

Saturated Fat: 3g

% Calories from Fat: 24

Carbohydrates: 8g

Protein: 16g

Cholesterol: 8mg

Sodium: 1139mg

Slice the polenta into ½-inch thick slices. Place the Steak Plate in the top of grill and the Grilling Plate in the bottom. Set the lever to the back. Set the temperature to High to allow the grill to preheat. When the green light goes off, the grill is preheated. Lightly brush the polenta slices with 1 teaspoon of oil and place on the Grilling Plate in a single layer. Close the lid. Grill for 2 to 3 minutes. Check the polenta and continue grilling until scored and golden brown.

In a medium saucepan, over medium-low heat, sauté the onion in the heated oil for 4 to 5 minutes, until softened and slightly caramelized. Add the zucchini, garlic, mushrooms, salt and pepper and sauté, stirring occasionally, until the vegetables are softened and slightly browned. Add the vegetable broth, tomato paste, canned tomatoes and basil, stirring to combine. Lower the heat and simmer for 8 to 10 minutes, stirring occasionally. The sauce will be thick. To serve, place several polenta slices on each individual plate and top with vegetable marinara.

Serves 4. ❧

*M*ARINADES, SAUCES AND RUBS are small additions offering tremendous, flavorful results when paired with grilled meats, poultry and fish. Fresh herbs, tangy spices, fresh vegetables, oils, vinegars and spicy flavorings created the recipes in this chapter and each is complementary to the wide variety of foods waiting to be prepared in your George Foreman® The Next Grilleration™ G5.

When choosing a healthful diet, look for lean cuts of meat and marinate each to add tenderness. Marinating breaks down the connective tissue in meat to act as a natural tenderizer. Marinades can be made well ahead of time and stored in an airtight container in the refrigerator until needed. Making the marinade in a resealable plastic bag adds to the ease of this preparation—just add the meat and reseal the bag. No mess!

Rubs and sauces are also easy to prepare, yet imbue meats, poultry and seafood with toothsome flavor. Rubs are a combination of herbs and spices and can be stored easily and used quickly to produce distinctive flavors. Create a paste from any rub by adding a small amount of oil or yogurt to the rub. This will create a more prominent crust, however, be sure to store any paste in the refrigerator until use. Sauces add moisture, which is important when grilling lean cuts of meat. They also add interest to the meal. Consider the *Western Smokey Bar-B-Que Sauce & Marinade,* which can be used for any cut of meat, poultry or fish! Outstanding flavors are just moments away when you prepare fresh marinades, rubs and sauces.

Old Orleans Marinade

A stout marinade that stands up to beef.

2 tablespoons	Worcestershire sauce
¼ cup	beef broth
¼ cup	low sodium soy sauce
1 teaspoon	ground paprika
1 teaspoon	dried thyme
1 teaspoon	black pepper
½ teaspoon	ground nutmeg
½ teaspoon	salt

Combine all the ingredients in a small bowl. Store any unused marinade in the refrigerator for up to 1 week.

Makes ¾ cup. ❧

Calories: 18

Total Fat: <1g

Saturated Fat: <1g

% Calories from Fat: 3

Carbohydrates: 2g

Protein: 1g

Cholesterol: <1mg

Sodium: 661mg

Mediterranean Marinade

The fresh flavors of Greece.

½ cup	fresh lemon juice
2 tablespoons	extra-virgin olive oil
¼ cup	white wine vinegar
¼ cup	green bell pepper, finely diced
2 tablespoons	fresh oregano, finely chopped
2 tablespoons	fresh parsley, finely chopped
2 cloves	fresh garlic, minced

Combine all the ingredients in a medium bowl. Store any unused marinade in an airtight container in the refrigerator for up to 1 week.

Makes 1¼ cups. ❧

Calories: 35

Total Fat: 3g

Saturated Fat: 0g

% Calories from Fat: 77

Carbohydrates: 2

Protein: <1g

Cholesterol: 0mg

Sodium: 1mg

Honey Mustard Marinade

Pungent mustard and sweet honey create a tangy, thick marinade.

2 tablespoons	honey
3 tablespoons	Dijon mustard
2 tablespoons	fresh lemon juice
1 tablespoon	extra-virgin olive oil
1 teaspoon	lemon pepper

Soften the honey in a microwave oven for 15 seconds. Combine all the ingredients and mix thoroughly into a thick paste. Brush on the chicken, pork, salmon or beef. Use immediately.

Makes ½ cup.

Calories: 80

Total Fat: 5g

Saturated Fat: <1g

% Calories from oFat: 48

Carbohydrates: 10g

Protein: <1g

Cholesterol: <1mg

Sodium: 64mg

Fiery Fruit Marinade

Especially great for fajitas.

½ cup	fresh lime juice
¼ cup	fresh orange juice
¼ cup	fresh papaya juice (substitute ¼ cup canned papaya juice)
¼ cup	prepared hot salsa
1 tablespoon	canola oil
2 tablespoons	fresh cilantro, chopped
1 teaspoon	ground cumin
1 teaspoon	salt

Combine all the ingredients in a medium bowl. Store any unused marinade in an airtight container in the refrigerator for up to 2 weeks.

Makes 1½ cups.

Calories: 20

Total Fat: 1g

Saturated Fat: <1g

% Calories from Fat: 51

Carbohydrates: 2g

Protein: <1g

Cholesterol: 0mg

Sodium: 223mg

Spicy Thai Marinade

Fresh lemongrass may be found in the produce aisle of your grocery store.

1 cup	lowfat coconut milk
2 tablespoons	fresh ginger, finely minced
1 stalk	lemongrass, chopped into large pieces
¼ cup	fresh cilantro, chopped
1 teaspoon	red pepper, crushed

Combine all the ingredients in a small saucepan and simmer over low heat for 5 minutes. Cool the marinade. Use immediately or store in an airtight container in the refrigerator for up to 1 week.

Makes 1 cup. ❧

Calories: 4
Total Fat: <1g
Saturated Fat: <1g
% Calories from Fat: 48
Carbohydrates: <1g
Protein: <1g
Cholesterol: 0mg
Sodium: 2mg

Monsoon Marinade

Flavors, color and texture create a complex marinade for chicken, beef, pork or fish.

1 cup	nonfat plain yogurt
¼	yellow onion, grated
2 tablespoons	fresh lemon juice
2 tablespoons	fresh cilantro, minced
2 cloves	garlic, minced
1 teaspoon	ground turmeric
½ teaspoon	ground cloves
1 teaspoon	black pepper
½ teaspoon	salt

Combine all the ingredients in a small bowl and use immediately.

Makes 1½ cups. ❧

Calories: 13
Total Fat: <1g
Saturated Fat: <1g
% Calories from Fat: 2
Carbohydrates: 2g
Protein: 1g
Cholesterol: <1mg
Sodium: 110mg

Maple-Orange Sauce

A sweet, tangy sauce that goes well with ham or pork chops.

1	shallot, finely minced
3 tablespoons	fresh orange juice concentrate
¼ cup	maple syrup
½ cup	water
2 tablespoons	low sodium soy sauce
¼ teaspoon	black pepper
1 tablespoon	cornstarch
2 tablespoons	cold water

In a small saucepan, combine all the ingredients except the cornstarch and water. Simmer over low heat for 2 minutes. Whisk the cornstarch into the water until dissolved and add to sauce, stirring until smooth. Simmer for an additional 5 minutes.

Makes 1 cup. ❧

Calories: 45

Total Fat: <1g

Saturated Fat: 0g

% Calories from Fat: <1

Carbohydrates: 11g

Protein: <1g

Cholesterol: 0mg

Sodium: 138mg

Grilled Vegetable Sauce

The healthiest sauce possible is great tossed with pasta, chicken, fish or serve chilled as a dip.

2 tablespoons	garlic olive oil
2 tablespoons	balsamic vinegar
1 teaspoon	dried basil
½ teaspoon	black pepper
½ teaspoon	salt
1 medium	zucchini, thinly sliced
1 medium	yellow squash, thinly sliced
1 small	purple onion, thinly sliced
1 medium	red bell pepper, cored, seeded and thinly sliced

Calories: 25

Total Fat: 2g

Saturated Fat: <1g

% Calories from Fat: 60

Carbohydrates: 2g

Protein: <1g

Cholesterol: 0mg

Sodium: 74mg

In a flat glass pan, combine the oil, vinegar, basil, pepper and salt. Add the vegetable slices, turning a few times to coat. Cover with plastic wrap and marinate in the refrigerator for 1 hour.

Place the Steak Plate in the top of the grill and the Grilling Plate in the bottom. Set the lever to the back. Set the temperature to High to allow the grill to preheat. When the green light goes off, the grill is preheated. Place the vegetables on the Grilling Plate in an even layer and close the lid. Cook for 4 minutes. Check the vegetables and continue cooking until softened and browned. Use a heat-resistant plastic spatula to transfer the vegetables to a food processor and blend until smooth, adding a few drips of water or oil, if necessary. Serve warmed or chilled.

Makes about 2 cups. ✑

Western Smokey Bar-B-Que Sauce & Marinade

A must with ribs, but also a winner with steak or chicken.

1 small	yellow onion, chopped
3 cloves	garlic, chopped
1 cup	prepared tomato sauce
¼ cup	apple cider vinegar
¼ cup	low sodium soy sauce
¼ cup	dark brown sugar
¼ cup	Worcestershire sauce
2 teaspoons	dry mustard
2 teaspoons	celery seed
1 teaspoon	bottled liquid smoke

Combine all of the ingredients in a small saucepan and simmer over medium heat for 8 to 10 minutes until slightly thickened. Cool the sauce. Use immediately or store in an airtight container in the refrigerator for up to 2 weeks.

Makes 2 cups. ❧

Calories: 29

Total Fat: <1g

Saturated Fat: <1g

% Calories from Fat: 21

Carbohydrates: 6g

Protein: 2g

Cholesterol: 0mg

Sodium: 240mg

Savory Herb Rub

A prefect way to perk up grilled fish or vegetables.

2 tablespoons	dried thyme
2 tablespoons	dried parsley
1 tablespoon	onion powder
2 tablespoons	garlic powder
1 tablespoon	ground paprika
1 tablespoon	black pepper
2 tablespoons	salt

Combine all the ingredients and mix thoroughly. Store in an airtight container in the refrigerator for up to 3 months.

Makes ¾ cup.

Calories: 19

Total Fat: <1g

Saturated Fat: <1g

% Calories from Fat: 7

Carbohydrates: 3g

Protein: <1g

Cholesterol: 0mg

Sodium: 1165mg

Rub de Provence

A lovely blend from the French area of Provence.

1 tablespoon	dried marjoram
1 tablespoon	dried thyme
1 tablespoon	dried savory
½ teaspoon	dried basil
½ teaspoon	dried rosemary
¼ teaspoon	dried lavender
¼ teaspoon	dried tarragon
¼ teaspoon	fennel seeds

Combine all the ingredients and mix thoroughly. Rub on chicken or fish or sprinkle into eggs or sauces. Store in an airtight container in the refrigerator for up to 3 months.

Makes ½ cup.

Calories: 19

Total Fat: <1g

Saturated Fat: <1g

% Calories from Fat: 13

Carbohydrates: 2g

Protein: <1g

Cholesterol: 0mg

Sodium: 1mg

Kasbah Spice Rub

An exotic and spicy rub for lamb, beef, chicken or pork.

3 tablespoons	ground paprika
1 tablespoon	ground coriander
1 tablespoon	ground cumin
1 tablespoon	ground turmeric
1 tablespoon	ground cardamom
2 teaspoons	ground ginger
2 teaspoons	ground cinnamon
1 teaspoon	black pepper
1 teaspoon	salt

Combine all the ingredients and mix thoroughly. Store in an airtight container in the refrigerator for up to 3 months.

Makes ½ cup. ❧

Calories: 45

Total Fat: 1g

Saturated Fat: <1g

% Calories from Fat: 23

Carbohydrates: 8g

Protein: 2g

Cholesterol: 0mg

Sodium: 588mg

Desserts

$\mathcal{E}$ VEN THE MOST FANTASTIC MEAL is made better with the addition of dessert. This special, sweet ending to any meal allows everyone to walk away from the meal satisfied. Dessert doesn't need to be served in large portions, nor does it need to be saturated in fats and sugar to be memorable. In this chapter, you'll find easy and rich-tasting desserts that don't tip the scales—*Tiramisu, Anjou Pears with Figs and Walnuts* and *Rustic Chocolate Panini*.

Fruit is an excellent choice for dessert when using the George Foreman® The Next Grilleration™ G5. Slice firm fruit (oranges, pineapple, mandarins, bananas, etc.) into slices ½-inch thick and warm in the grill for 2 to 3 minutes. When warmed, fruit juices are released and sweet flavors abound! Serve over lowfat pound cake or frozen yogurt.

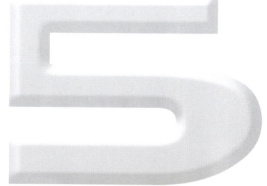

Grilled Tropical Trifle

Great Britain collides with the tropics for a sweet and luscious desert.

4 slices	angel food cake, 1-inch thick
4	fresh pineapple slices (substitute canned slices, if desired)
1	banana, peeled and chopped
2 cups	prepared reduced calorie vanilla pudding
1	mango, thinly sliced
2	kiwi, peeled and thinly sliced
4 teaspoons	coconut, shredded
4 teaspoons	Macadamia nuts, chopped

Place the Steak Plate in the top of the grill and the Grilling Plate in the bottom. Set the lever to the back. Set the temperature to Medium to allow the grill to preheat. When the green light goes off, the grill is preheated. Place the angel food cake slices on the Grilling Plate and close the lid. Cook for 2 minutes. Remove the cake and place the pineapple slices on the Grilling Plate. Close the lid and cook for 2 minutes.

Mix the banana with the vanilla pudding. To serve, place a pineapple slice on each plate and top with 1 piece of grilled cake. Spoon one-fourth of the banana pudding over the cake and arrange the mango and kiwi slices on top in a fan shape, alternating the mango and kiwi. Sprinkle with the shredded coconut and nuts.

Serves 4. ❧

Calories: 333

Total Fat: 4g

Saturated Fat: 1g

% Calories from Fat: 11

Carbohydrates: 73g

Protein: 5g

Cholesterol: 1mg

Sodium: 386mg

Rustic Chocolate Panini

A simple desert—so simple that you can prepare every night of the week!

4 slices	rustic French bread, ½-inch thick
4 teaspoons	lowfat margarine
3 ounces	semi-sweet chocolate chips

Spread the margarine on the outside of each slice of bread. Place each slice buttered side down on a clean surface. Top 2 bread slices with half of the chips, leaving a margin of space around the edges. Cover with a second slice of bread, buttered side up.

Place the Steak Plate in the top of the grill and the Grilling Plate in the bottom. Set the lever to the back. Set the temperature to Medium to allow the grill to preheat. When the green light goes off, the grill is preheated. Place the panini on the Grilling Plate and close the lid. Cook for 2 minutes or until the chocolate is melted. Cool slightly and cut each piece in half before serving.

Serves 4. ❧

Calories: 362

Total Fat: 9g

Saturated Fat: 4g

% Calories from Fat: 11

Carbohydrates: 64g

Protein: 10g

Cholesterol: 0mg

Sodium: 622mg

Orange Cinnamon-Raisin Panini

A sweet treat that your family and friends will love!

4 ounces	lowfat cream cheese
1 tablespoon	dark brown sugar
½ teaspoon	almond extract
4 slices	cinnamon-raisin bread, ½-inch thick
4 teaspoons	lowfat margarine
2 small	oranges, peeled and thinly sliced

In a small bowl combine the cream cheese, sugar and almond extract, mixing well to blend. Spread the margarine on the outside of the bread slices and place, buttered side down, on a clean surface. Spread a layer of the cream cheese mixture on each of the 4 bread slices. Place the orange slices on top of the cream cheese on 2 slices of bread and cover each with a second slice of bread.

Place the Steak Plate in the top of the grill and the Baking Pan in the bottom. Set the lever to the back. Set the temperature to Medium to allow the grill to preheat. When the green light goes off, the grill is preheated. Place the panini in the Baking Pan and close the lid. Cook for 2 minutes or until the cheese is warm and the outside is golden brown. Cool slightly and cut each piece in half before serving.

Serves 4. ❧

Calories: 188

Total Fat: 9g

Saturated Fat: 5g

% Calories from Fat: 24

Carbohydrates: 18g

Protein: 6g

Cholesterol: 21mg

Sodium: 247mg

Tiramisu

The sweetened mascarpone melts into a luscious, gooey filling that tastes of chocolate and coffee, creating an incredible treat. This traditional Italian pudding is heavy in fat, so enjoy only occasionally. Mascarpone is available in the specialty cheese case at your super market.

2 cups	mascarpone cheese
½ cup	powdered sugar
¼ cup	espresso powder, divided
2 tablespoons	cocoa powder
½ cup	prepared lowfat vanilla pudding
4 slices	pound cake, 1-inch thick
¼ cup	strong coffee
1 cup	nonfat whipped cream topping
	cocoa powder for dusting

Calories: 721

Total Fat: 54g

Saturated Fat: <1g

% Calories from Fat: 66

Carbohydrates: 52g

Protein: 9g

Cholesterol: 156mg

Sodium: 217mg

In a medium bowl, combine the mascarpone, sugar, espresso powder, 2 tablespoons of cocoa powder and the vanilla pudding, mixing well to blend. Very lightly brush one side of the cake with the coffee. Spread a layer of the cheese mixture on 2 slices of the cake, leaving a space around the edges and place a dollop of pudding in the center. Cover each with a second slice of cake.

Place the Steak Plate in the top of the grill and the Grilling Plate in the bottom. Set the lever to the back. Set the temperature to Medium to allow the grill to preheat. When the green light goes off, the grill is preheated. Place the cake slices on the Grilling Plate and close the lid. Cook for 1 to 2 minutes. Use a heat-resistant plastic spatula to transfer the Tiramisu to dessert plates and cool slightly. Top with the remaining sweetened mascarpone-pudding mixture, whipped cream and cocoa powder.

Serves 4. ❧

Anjou Pears with Figs and Walnuts

A simple desert that may be assembled ahead of time and grilled just before serving.

2 small	ripe Anjou pears
4	dried figs, chopped
⅛ teaspoon	ground coriander
¼ teaspoon	ground cinnamon
2 tablespoons	honey
1 teaspoon	dark brown sugar
¼ cup	walnuts, chopped

Peel the pears, cut in half lengthwise, and core. In a small bowl, combine the figs, coriander, cinnamon, honey, brown sugar and walnuts, mixing well to blend. Pack a spoonful of the sweetened fig-nut mixture into the "cup" created when coring the pear.

Place the Steak Plate in the top of the grill and the Baking Pan in the bottom. Set the lever to the back. Set the temperature to Medium to allow the grill to preheat. When the green light goes off, the grill is preheated. Place the pears, cut side up, in the Baking Pan and close the lid. Cook for 2½ to 3 minutes or until the pears are tender. Continue cooking for 1 minute, if necessary. Serve the pears topped with a scoop of lowfat vanilla-bean frozen yogurt.

Serves 4. ❧

Calories: 180

Total Fat: 5g

Saturated Fat: <1g

% Calories from Fat: 23

Carbohydrates: 35g

Protein: 3g

Cholesterol: 0mg

Sodium: 3mg

Chai Banana Shortcake

Berries out of season? You won't even miss them!

2	ripe bananas, peeled
¼ cup	fresh orange juice
1 teaspoon	orange zest
2 tablespoons	dark brown sugar
¼ teaspoon	ground cardamom
2 tablespoons	pecans, chopped
4	packaged shortcakes (substitute 4 slices lowfat pound cake)
2 cups	nonfat whipped cream topping

Cut the bananas in half lengthwise. In a small bowl, combine the orange juice, orange zest, brown sugar, cardamom and pecans. Place the Steak Plate in the top of the grill and the Grilling Plate in the bottom. Set the lever to the back. Set the temperature to Medium to allow the grill to preheat. When the green light goes off, the grill is preheated. Place the bananas on the Grilling Plate and liberally spoon the chai glaze down the center of each banana half. Close the lid. Cook for 1 minute or until the bananas are softened. Continue grilling for 1 minute, if necessary. To serve, place the shortcake on individual plates. Cut the banana slices in half crosswise and place 2 pieces on top of each shortcake. Drizzle with any glaze that has melted into the drip tray during cooking and mound with whipped cream.

Serves 4. ❧

Calories: 253

Total Fat: 3g

Saturated Fat: <1g

% Calories from Fat: 12

Carbohydrates: 52g

Protein: 3g

Cholesterol: 0mg

Sodium: 120mg

Chocolate Chip Cookies

The George Foreman® The Next Grilleration™ G5 bakes everyone's favorite
cookie without heating up the kitchen.

2½ cups	all-purpose flour
1 teaspoon	baking soda
1 cup	lowfat margarine, softened
¾ cup	packed brown sugar
½ cup	white granulated sugar
2	eggs
1 teaspoon	vanilla extract
12 ounce	package semisweet chocolate chip morsels

In a medium bowl, mix together the flour and baking soda. In a large bowl, place the softened margarine and sugars and beat with an electric mixer until light and fluffy. Add the eggs and vanilla and beat until combined, scraping down the sides of the bowl with a rubber spatula. Gradually add the flour mixture and mix until a smooth batter forms. Remove the electric mixer and fold in the chocolate chips using a large spoon.

Place the Steak Plate in the top of grill and the Baking Pan in the bottom. Set the lever to the back. Set the temperature to Medium to allow the grill to preheat. When the green light goes off, the grill is preheated. Drop the cookies by teaspoons, 2 inches apart, in the Baking Pan and flatten the top of each cookie by pressing down with the back of a spoon. Close the lid and bake the cookies for 6 to 8 minutes. Carefully slip a flat, heat-resistant plastic spatula completely under each cookie and transfer to a large plate. The cookies will be very soft, but will crisp nicely as they cool. Repeat with the remaining cookie dough.

Makes about 40 cookies, 2 cookies per serving. ❧

Calories: 225

Total Fat: 8g

Saturated Fat: 4g

% Calories from Fat: 31

Carbohydrates: 36g

Protein: 3g

Cholesterol: 24mg

Sodium: 179mg

chapter nine

Basic Cooking Guide

Food	Grilling Minutes	Temp.	Notes
Beef			
Flank steak	6-7	Med	Sliced thinly to serve
Hamburger, 4 oz.	3-5	Med	
8 oz.	4-6	Med	
Kebabs	5-7	Med	1 inch pieces
London broil	6-7	High	1½-2 inches thick
Ribeye	5-7	High	
Ribs, Short ribs	7-8	Med	Parboil prior to grilling
Loin ribs	6-7	Med	Parboil prior to grilling
Round steak	3-4	High	
Sirloin	5-6	High	
T-Bone	5-6	High	
Tenderloin	4-6	High	
Fruit			
Apple	2-3	Med	½-inch slices cored, cut in half, lengthwise
Bananas	1-2	Med	sliced lengthwise
Nectarines	1-2	Med	cut in half or sliced
Peaches	1-2	Med	cut in half or sliced
Pineapple	2-3	Med	½-inch thick slices

Food	Grilling Minutes	Temp.	Notes
Lamb			
Ground lamb	6-7	Med	
Kebabs	6-8	Med	1-inch pieces
Loin chops	4-6	Med	
Pork			
Bacon	10-13	High	Baking Pan
Bacon	7-8	High	Grilling Plate
Center cut chops	4-5	Med	½-inch thick
Ground pork	5-7	Med	
Ham	2-4	Med	fully cooked, ½-inch thick slice
Kebabs	6-7	Med	1-inch pieces
Loin chops	4-5	Med	½-inch thick
Ribs, Baby back ribs	4-6	Med	Parboil prior to grilling
Country style ribs	7-9	Med	boneless
Sausage	4-6	Med	lowfat, link or patty style
Tenderloin	4-6	Med	
Poultry			
Chicken breasts	6-8	Med	boneless/skinless
Chicken kebabs	6-8	Med	1-inch pieces
Chicken sausage	6-8	Med	lowfat, link or patty style
Chicken thighs	6-7	High	
Ground turkey	8-9	Med	
Turkey breast, boneless/skinless			
Thin sliced	4-5	Med	
Sliced	6-8	Med	¼-½ inch thick
Sandwiches			
Cheese	2-3	High	
Tuna Melt	3-4	Med	

Food	Grilling Minutes	Temp.	Notes
Sandwiches			
Ham	2-3	High	
Roast Beef	2-3	High	
Rueben	3-4	Med	
Sausage	2-3	High	
Turkey	3-4	Med	
Seafood			
Halibut steak	6-8	Med	½-1 inch thick
Kebabs	6-8	Med	1-inch pieces
Mahi Mahi fillet	3-5	Med	
Orange Roughy fillet	3-5	Med	
Red Snapper fillet	3-5	Med	
Salmon, Fillet	5-8	Med	1-inch thick
Steak	5-8	Med	½-1 inch thick
Scallops	4-6	Med	
Sea Bass fillet	3-5	Med	
Shrimp-Medium	1½-2½	High	
Swordfish steak	7-9	High	1-1½ inch thick
Trout	3-5	Med	
Tuna steak	5-7	High	½-1 inch thick
Snacks (Frozen)			
Single Serving Pizza (7-inch)	8-10	Med	Baking Pan
French Fries - reg cut	12-14	High	Baking Pan
crinkle cut	14-16	High	Baking Pan
Chicken nuggets	5-7	High	Baking Pan
Mini Quiche	12-14	Med	Baking Pan
Burrito	8-10	Med	Baking Pan
Taquitos	6-8	High	Baking Pan

Food	Grilling Minutes	Temp.	Notes
Vegetables			
Asparagus	4-5	Med	lengthwise (vertically) on grill
Brussels sprouts	8-10	Med	frozen, thawed
Carrots	6-8	Med	¼-½ inch thick slices
Eggplant	8-10	Med	¼-½ inch thick slices or cubed
Onions	2-3	High	thinly sliced
Onions	3-4	High	thick sliced
Peppers	4-5	High	thinly sliced
Peppers	7-9	Med	1-inch chunks
Potatoes, Baking	7-8	High	¼-½ inch thick slices or cubed
Red	7-8	High	¼-½ inch thick slices or cubed
Sweet	7-8	High	¼-½ inch thick slices or cubed
Squash	7-9	Med	¼-½ inch thick slices or cubed

Index

*A*bacore Tuna Melt, 46

Anjou Pears with Figs & Walnuts, 111

Apples, 114

Apple Ginger Waffles, 26

Artichoke Stuffed Chicken, 83

Asparagus, 117

Avocado & Crab Quesadilla, 49

*B*acon, 115

Bacon & Eggs, Your Way, 16

Breakfast Tacos, 17

Grilled Bacon-Wrapped Shrimp, 9

Omelet Lorraine, 18

Bananas, 114

Chai Banana Shortcake, 112

Grilled Tropical Trifle, 107

Beef, 114

Beef Medallions with Tomatillo Pesto, 69

Grilled Beef with Root Vegetables &
  Orange Vinaigrette, 54

Korean Barbeque, 72

Red Flannel Hash, 20

Steak & Potato Panini, 41

Stuffed Flank Steak, 70

Tenderloin Steaks with Grilled Mushrooms
  & Blue Cheese, 71

Beets

Grilled Beef with Root Vegetables &
  Orange Vinaigrette, 54

Red Flannel Hash, 20

Biscuits, Fresh Home-Baked, 21

Blackberries

Croissant French Toast with Warm Berries, 35

Sour Cream Blackberry Waffles, 25

Blueberries

Croissant French Toast with Warm Berries, 35

Bread. *See Biscuits; Crostini; French toast; Muffins;
  Pancakes; Panini; Sandwiches; Tortillas; Waffles*

Breakfast Rice Cakes, 32

Breakfast Tacos, 17

Brussels sprouts, 117

Buckwheat Pancakes with Strawberries
  & Cream, 31

Buttermilk Pancakes, 30

*C*alzone, Grilled Vegetable, 48

Caper-Dill Waffles with Smoked Salmon
  Cream Cheese, 27

Capresi Panini, 39

Caribbean Lamb with Mint Yogurt Sauce, 73

Carrots, 117

Lemon-Honey Glazed Carrots, 65

Chai Banana Shortcake, 112

Chevre, Fig & Prosciutto Panini, 40

Chicken, 115

Artichoke Stuffed Chicken, 83

Chicken & Gruyere Quesadilla, 50

Chicken Piccata, 86

Crispy Baked Chicken, 82

Greek Chicken Orzo Salad, 52

Grilled Chicken Mole, 81

Sun-Dried Tomato Chicken & Zucchini
  with Penne, 87

Chiles

Chipotle Mayonnaise, 38

Crab & Avocado Quesadilla, 49

Stuffed Chile Rellenos, 93

Chipotle Mayonnaise, 38

Chocolate

Chocolate Chip Cookies, 113

Rustic Chocolate Panini, 108

Tiramisu, 110

Cleaning tips, 6

Coffee

Tiramisu, 110

Cookies, Chocolate Chip, 113

Cooking guide, 114–17

Corn Cakes, Curried, 8

Cornmeal Muffins, 23

Couscous, Moroccan, Paprika Game
Hens with, 84

Crab

Crab & Avocado Quesadilla, 49

Maryland Crab Cakes, 91

Cranberry-Orange, Smoked Turkey & Edam
Panini, 42

Crispy Baked Chicken, 82

Crispy Hash Browned Potatoes, 22

Croissant French Toast with Warm Berries, 35

Croque Monsieur, 44

Crostini, Homemade Grilled, 12

Cuban Sandwich, 44

Curried Corn Cakes, 8

esserts

Anjou Pears with Figs & Walnuts, 111

Chai Banana Shortcake, 112

Chocolate Chip Cookies, 113

Grilled Tropical Trifle, 107

Orange Cinnamon-Raisin Panini, 109

Rustic Chocolate Panini, 108

Tiramisu, 110

Dijon Lemon Oysters with Angel Hair
Pasta, 92

Dijon Mushroom Stuffed Pork Chops, 77

Duo Olive Tapenade, 39

ggplant, 117

Eggplant Parmesan Focaccia, 43

Grilled Japanese Vegetables with
Wasabi Butter, 66

Spinach Stuffed Eggplant, 95

Eggs or egg substitute

Bacon & Eggs, Your Way, 16

Breakfast Tacos, 17

Migas, 19

Omelet Lorraine, 18

Simply Scrambled Eggs, 15

ajitas, Grilled Swordfish, 89

Fiery Fruit Marinade, 99

Figs

Anjou Pears with Figs & Walnuts, 111

Chevre, Fig & Prosciutto Panini, 40

Fish, 116

Albacore Tuna Melt, 46

Caper-Dill Waffles with Smoked Salmon
Cream Cheese, 27

Grilled & Chilled Seafood Salad, 53

Grilled Swordfish Fajitas, 89

Herb-Crusted Salmon with Yellow Tomato
Relish, 90

Pacific Rim Salmon Steaks, 88

Focaccia, Eggplant Parmesan, 43

French toast
Croissant French Toast with Warm Berries, 35
French Toast with Strawberry Butter, 33
Pecan Orange Stuffed French Toast, 34
Fresh Home-Baked Biscuits, 21

Fruit, 106, 114. *See also individual fruits*
Fiery Fruit Marinade, 99
Grilled Tropical Trifle, 107

Game Hens, Paprika, with Moroccan
Couscous, 84
Garlic
Grilled Garlic & Potato Salad, 55
Homemade Grilled Crostini, 12
Lemon Garlic Spread, 37
Greek Chicken Orzo Salad, 52
Greek Olive & Lamb in Pita, 47
Grilled & Chilled Seafood Salad, 53
Grilled Bacon-Wrapped Shrimp, 9
Grilled Beef with Root Vegetables &
Orange Vinaigrette, 54
Grilled Chicken Mole, 81
Grilled Garlic & Potato Salad, 55
Grilled Garnet Yams with Fruit &
Spiced Butter, 67
Grilled Japanese Vegetables with
Wasabi Butter, 66
Grilled Polenta with Duo Olive Tapenade, 13
Grilled Polenta with Vegetable Marinara, 96
Grilled Swordfish Fajitas, 89
Grilled Teriyaki Tofu, 94
Grilled Tropical Trifle, 107
Grilled Vegetable Calzone, 48

Grilled Vegetable Sauce, 102
Grilling tips, 5–6

Halibut, 116
Grilled & Chilled Seafood Salad, 53
Ham, 115
Chevre, Fig & Prosciutto Panini, 40
Croque Monsieur, 44
Cuban Sandwich, 44
Hash, Red Flannel, 20
Hash Browned Potatoes, Crispy, 22
Herb-Crusted Salmon with Yellow
Tomato Relish, 90
Homemade Grilled Crostini, 12
Honey Mustard Marinade, 99
Hot Sausage & Peppers Sandwich, 45

Island Jerked Pork with Lime Crème
Fraîche, 75

Kasbah Spice Rub, 105
Kebabs, 114, 115, 116
Keema Kebabs with Mango Chutney
Dipping Sauce, 10
Korean Barbeque, 72

Lamb, 115
Caribbean Lamb with Mint Yogurt Sauce, 73
Greek Olive & Lamb in Pita, 47
Keema Kebabs with Mango Chutney
Dipping Sauce, 10
Lamb Chops Stuffed with Greek Gremolata, 74

Lemons
Lemon Garlic Spread, 37
Lemon-Honey Glazed Carrots, 65
Mediterranean Marinade, 98

*M*angoes
Crab & Avocado Quesadilla, 49
Grilled Tropical Trifle, 107
Mango Chutney Dipping Sauce, 11
Maple-Orange Sauce, 101
Marinades, 97
Fiery Fruit Marinade, 99
Honey Mustard Marinade, 99
Mediterranean Marinade, 98
Monsoon Marinade, 100
Old Orleans Marinade, 98
Spicy Thai Marinade, 100
Western Smokey Bar-B-Que Sauce &
Marinade, 103
Maryland Crab Cakes, 91
Mayonnaise
Chipotle Mayonnaise, 38
Quick Dijonaise Sauce, 38
Mediterranean Marinade, 98
Migas, 19
Mint Yogurt Sauce, 73
Monsoon Marinade, 100
Muffins, Cornmeal, 23
Mushrooms
Chicken & Gruyere Quesadilla, 50
Dijon Mushroom Stuffed Pork Chops, 77
Grilled Polenta with Vegetable Marinara, 96
Grilled Vegetable Calzone, 48
Stuffed Flank Steak, 70

Tenderloin Steaks with Grilled Mushrooms &
Blue Cheese, 71

*N*ectarines, 114

*O*atmeal Cinnamon Raisin Pancakes, 28
Old Orleans Marinade, 98
Olives
Duo Olive Tapenade, 39
Greek Olive & Lamb in Pita, 47
Omelet Lorraine, 18
Onions, 117
Oranges
Grilled Garnet Yams with Fruit &
Spiced Butter, 67
Maple-Orange Sauce, 101
Orange Cinnamon-Raisin Panini, 109
Orange Pecan Cream Cheese, 34
Pecan Orange Stuffed French Toast, 34
Oysters, Dijon Lemon, with Angel Hair
Pasta, 92

*P*acific Rim Salmon Steaks, 88
Pancakes
Buckwheat Pancakes with Strawberries
& Cream, 31
Buttermilk Pancakes, 30
Oatmeal Cinnamon Raisin Pancakes, 28
Pumpkin Soufflé Pancakes, 29
Panini
Capresi Panini, 39
Chevre, Fig & Prosciutto Panini, 40
Eggplant Parmesan Focaccia, 43

Orange Cinnamon-Raisin Panini, 109

Rustic Chocolate Panini, 108

Smoked Turkey, Edam & Orange-
Cranberry Panini, 42

Steak & Potato Panini, 41

Paprika Game Hens with Moroccan
Couscous, 84

Pasta

Dijon Lemon Oysters with Angel Hair
Pasta, 92

Greek Chicken Orzo Salad, 52

Spinach Stuffed Eggplant, 95

Sun-Dried Tomato Chicken & Zucchini
with Penne, 87

Peaches, 114

Pears, Anjou, with Figs & Walnuts, 111

Pecans

Orange Pecan Cream Cheese, 34

Pecan Orange Stuffed French Toast, 34

Peppers, 117

Grilled & Chilled Seafood Salad, 53

Grilled Swordfish Fajitas, 89

Hot Sausage & Peppers Sandwich, 45

Yukon Ranch Potatoes, 56

Perfect Morning Waffles, 24

Pineapple, 114

Grilled Bacon-Wrapped Shrimp, 9

Grilled Garnet Yams with Fruit & Spiced
Butter, 67

Grilled Tropical Trifle, 107

Polenta

Grilled Polenta with Duo Olive Tapenade, 13

Grilled Polenta with Vegetable Marinara, 96

Pork, 115

Cuban Sandwich, 44

Dijon Mushroom Stuffed Pork Chops, 77

Island Jerked Pork with Lime Crème
Fraîche, 75

Pork Tenderloin with Quick Raspberry
Sauce, 76

Santa Fe Pork Ribs, 78

Potatoes, 117

Breakfast Tacos, 17

Crispy Hash Browned Potatoes, 22

Grilled Garlic & Potato Salad, 55

Red Flannel Hash, 20

Steak & Potato Panini, 41

Yukon Ranch Potatoes, 56

Prosciutto. *See Ham*

Pumpkin Soufflé Pancakes, 29

Quesadillas

Chicken & Gruyere Quesadilla, 50

Crab & Avocado Quesadilla, 49

Quick Dijonaise Sauce, 38

Raspberries

Croissant French Toast with Warm
Berries, 35

Pork Tenderloin with Quick Raspberry
Sauce, 76

Red Flannel Hash, 20

Rice

Breakfast Rice Cakes, 32

Stuffed Chile Rellenos, 93

Rubs, 97

Kasbah Spice Rub, 105

Rub de Provence, 104

Savory Herb Rub, 104

Rustic Chocolate Panini, 108

alads

Greek Chicken Orzo Salad, 52

Grilled & Chilled Seafood Salad, 53

Grilled Beef with Root Vegetables & Orange Vinaigrette, 54

Grilled Garlic & Potato Salad, 55

Salmon, 116

Caper-Dill Waffles with Smoked Salmon Cream Cheese, 27

Herb-Crusted Salmon with Yellow Tomato Relish, 90

Pacific Rim Salmon Steaks, 88

Sandwiches, 115–16. *See also Panini; Quesadillas*

Albacore Tuna Melt, 46

Croque Monsieur, 44

Cuban Sandwich, 44

Greek Olive & Lamb in Pita, 47

Hot Sausage & Peppers Sandwich, 45

Santa Fe Pork Ribs, 78

Sauces, 97

Grilled Vegetable Sauce, 102

Mango Chutney Dipping Sauce, 11

Maple-Orange Sauce, 101

Mint Yogurt Sauce, 73

Quick Dijonaise Sauce, 38

Western Smokey Bar-B-Que Sauce & Marinade, 103

Sausage, 115

Breakfast Tacos, 17

Hot Sausage & Peppers Sandwich, 45

Savory Herb Rub, 104

Scallops, 116

Grilled & Chilled Seafood Salad, 53

Shortcake, Chai Banana, 112

Shrimp, 116

Grilled & Chilled Seafood Salad, 53

Grilled Bacon-Wrapped Shrimp, 9

Simple Lemon Thyme Turkey, 85

Simply Scrambled Eggs, 15

Smoked Turkey, Edam & Orange-Cranberry Panini, 42

Snacks, frozen, 116

Sour Cream Blackberry Waffles, 25

Spicy Thai Marinade, 100

Spinach Stuffed Eggplant, 95

Spreads

Duo Olive Tapenade, 39

Lemon Garlic Spread, 37

Tuscan Tomato Spread, 37

Squash, 117. *See also Zucchini*

Grilled Japanese Vegetables with Wasabi Butter, 66

Grilled Vegetable Sauce, 102

Steak & Potato Panini, 41

Strawberries

Buckwheat Pancakes with Strawberries & Cream, 31

Strawberry Butter, 33

Stuffed Chile Rellenos, 93

Stuffed Flank Steak, 70

Sun-Dried Tomato Chicken & Zucchini with Penne, 87

Swordfish, 116

Grilled Swordfish Fajitas, 89

Tacos, Breakfast, 17

Tapenade, Duo Olive, 39

Tenderloin Steaks with Grilled Mushrooms & Blue Cheese, 71

Tiramisu, 110
Tofu, Grilled Teriyaki, 94
Tomatillo Pesto, Beef Medallions with, 69
Tomatoes
  Capresi Panini, 39
  Grilled Polenta with Vegetable Marinara, 96
  Herb-Crusted Salmon with Yellow
    Tomato Relish, 90
  Stuffed Flank Steak, 70
  Sun-Dried Tomato Chicken & Zucchini
    with Penne, 87
  Tuscan Tomato Spread, 37
  Western Smokey Bar-B-Que Sauce &
    Marinade, 103
Tortilla chips
  Migas, 19
Tortillas
  Breakfast Tacos, 17
  Chicken & Gruyere Quesadilla, 50
  Crab & Avocado Quesadilla, 49
  Grilled Swordfish Fajitas, 89
Trifle, Grilled Tropical, 107
Tuna, 116
  Albacore Tuna Melt, 46
Turkey, 79, 115
  Simple Lemon Thyme Turkey, 85
  Smoked Turkey, Edam & Orange-
    Cranberry Panini, 42
Tuscan Tomato Spread, 37

egetables, 51, 117. *See also
  individual vegetables*
Grilled Beef with Root Vegetables &
  Orange Vinaigrette, 54

Grilled Japanese Vegetables with
  Wasabi Butter, 66
Grilled Polenta with Vegetable Marinara, 96
Grilled Vegetable Calzone, 48
Grilled Vegetable Sauce, 102

*W*affles
Apple Ginger Waffles, 26
Caper-Dill Waffles with Smoked Salmon
  Cream Cheese, 27
Perfect Morning Waffles, 24
Sour Cream Blackberry Waffles, 25
Walnuts, Anjou Pears with Figs &, 111
Western Smokey Bar-B-Que Sauce &
  Marinade, 103

*Y*ams, Grilled Garnet, with Fruit &
  Spiced Butter, 67
Yogurt
  Mint Yogurt Sauce, 73
  Monsoon Marinade, 100
Yukon Ranch Potatoes, 56

*Z*ucchini
  Grilled Polenta with Vegetable Marinara, 96
  Grilled Vegetable Calzone, 48
  Grilled Vegetable Sauce, 102
  Sun-Dried Tomato Chicken & Zucchini
    with Penne, 87